# ACCLAIM FOR *PURPOSE* ...

MW00627814

"Wilkins dives deep to marry life and business philosophies into practical strategies, unique equations, and tactical solutions to live your most purpose-forward life."

—Peter Barris, Chair, New Enterprise Associates (NEA)

"What does it mean to be a Purpose First Entrepreneur? Wilkins goes so far beyond revenue or bottom lines and redefines what we think of as a 'successful' business. Thoughtful, engaging, and inspiring. A must-read for future entrepreneurs."

—Tobias J. Moskowitz, Dean Takahashi Professor of Finance, Yale School of Management

"The new future of entrepreneurship has arrived, and it starts with purpose."

—Andy Friedman, Founder, SkinnyPop Popcorn

"Wilkins captures the essence of creating a life and business that matters: you must first have purpose."

—Katlin Smith, Founder & CEO, Simple Mills

"Being a kick-ass entrepreneur doesn't mean getting your ass kicked. *Purpose First Entrepreneur* goes beyond business and teaches you how to live well."

—Garry Cooper, CEO & Co-Founder, Rheaply

"In a world of entrepreneurship, no one is talking about the key to true success: purpose. Wilkins homes in on his secret weapon and shows you, too, how to be a Purpose First Entrepreneur."

—Betsy Ziegler, CEO, 1871

"From the vantage point of overcoming overwhelming adversity and running one of the top early-stage investment groups in the country, Pete Wilkins provides a purposeful framework that can help you achieve entrepreneurial and overall success."

—Steven N. Kaplan, Neubauer Family Distinguished Service Professor of Entrepreneurship and Finance, University of Chicago Booth School of Business, and Kessenich E.P. Faculty Director at the Polsky Center of Entrepreneurship and Innovation, University of Chicago

"Supercharge your start-up with Purpose. Pete gives you all the tools you need."

—Scott Issen, Co-Founder & CEO, Future Founders

"Wish I had this book when I started out! *Purpose First Entrepreneur* helps troubleshoot and avoid common personal and professional pitfalls along the entrepreneurship path."

—Amanda Lannert, CEO, Jellyvision

"Pete brings incredible focus, positive energy, and a deep sense of purpose to help entrepreneurs succeed against the odds."

—John Lewis, Executive Partner, Madison Dearborn, and Executive Chairman, InMoment

"I met Pete when I was fundraising for my business, and I was struck most by the energy he had for the people who created it. Pete didn't invest in my business, but he did something even better, he poured time, effort, and hours into me as an entrepreneur, which I'd take over his money any day. Whether you're just starting down the path to entrepreneurship, you're approaching burn-out, or you're losing touch with your 'why,' *Purpose First Entrepreneur* has something for you."

—Jeana Anderson Cohen, Founder & CEO, aSweatLife

# PURPOSE + FIRST

# ENTREPRENEUR

**Discover Your Purpose**
**Turn It into a Thriving Business**
**Perform at an Elite Level**

## PETE WILKINS

OMAXEN
PUBLISHING

# CONTENTS

# INTRODUCTION

I was a hopeful, scrappy kid.

I grew up in a three-bedroom house with three brothers, three sisters, my parents, and my grandmother. As you can imagine, there was *never* any quiet in my life. I learned to survive as much as I did thrive, and life was an exciting mix of noise, constant demands, love, motion, and change. I believed I was invincible (heck, with six brothers and sisters beating me up, I pretty much was), but more than that, I had this feeling that things would always stay the same … like it didn't matter what we didn't have, because we had each other.

One night, when I was ten, my sister woke me up. She told me that my mom had died in her sleep. We'd brought her home from the hospital a few days earlier as the doctors told us she had lost her battle with cancer and there was nothing more they could do. I ran downstairs, looked out the window, and saw my mom being wheeled out by the funeral director.

For as long as I live, I don't believe that image will ever leave my mind, because in that one singular moment, everything I knew about life changed. The known was now *un*known. Without realizing it at the time, that is where my quest for purpose emerged. (And for so many of us, the unknown presents challenges, both personally and professionally, especially today.)

After my mother's death, I struggled. I acted out in school. I was aimless. My father finally decided to send me to the local Catholic school to give me some direction. It was tough because we didn't have the money, but he was willing to make that sacrifice. Though school didn't start off well, I finally settled down and started to heal. My faith started to put purpose back in my life. Over time, my relationship with my father grew stronger and stronger. He taught me so much and instilled values that allowed me to flourish in high school.

My life, once again, had purpose.

Then, when things were finally on an upswing, I got a phone call. I picked up the phone and heard, "Pete, Dad's had a stroke. We found him dead on the couch at home. There was nothing we could do."

I was in complete and utter shock.

When you're a teenager and both your parents are dead, it's hard to make sense of life. Even now, the recent pandemic has created mass personal and economic loss, which is tied so closely to identity. As we lose our jobs, our health, or our sense of safety or freedom, that's when things really start to unravel. Who do we become without our loved ones, our comfort zones, or our safety nets?

Feeling like I didn't know who I was, I quit my college football team, even though I'd just earned a scholarship as a walk-on, and decided to transfer colleges. I was miserable, and I wanted the pain and hurt to stop. I had nowhere to turn, so I started doing anything I could that would take my mind off the pain—especially drinking.

I needed a new start, but instead of taking action, I became numb.

While visiting my hometown, I decided to attend a party with a group of close friends. It was December 23, and the next day,

I was going to celebrate Christmas Eve with my family. Shortly after we arrived, some notoriously bad dudes showed up looking for trouble. Within minutes, a fight broke out. My friend got hit and fell to the floor. I went to help, and as I tried to pull him up, someone cracked me in the side of the head with a solid wooden coat-tree that bore the force of a baseball player swinging a bat at a 100-mph fastball.

The blow shattered my skull and punctured an artery in my brain. Blood gushed from the open wound as I fell to the floor. I was rushed to the emergency room, and the doctors told my friends and family to hope for a miracle. After two brain surgeries—one that required a plate in my skull—I had an arduous recovery. I had to learn how to walk, talk, and cognitively function again. It was a miracle I even survived.

During that time, I questioned everything I knew about life and what I was supposed to even do or feel. I'd lost my mother, my father, my sport, and now, my identity. Who was I if I couldn't walk or talk? How would I ever find the strength to recover when I felt I had so little to live for?

There's something about loss that shapes you; it changes the way you react, interact, and even feel about the day-to-day. My entire young life went from revolving around enjoying myself to losing both parents to almost dying before my life had really begun.

As I recovered from that attack, I had a choice: I could give in to the whims of my tragic life, or I could create something from it. And that's what I did. Through a hell of a lot of rehab, therapy, and perseverance, I decided to carve out a new purpose from the old.

Today, you might be asking yourself about your purpose. Perhaps you haven't faced death, but you might be able to relate to wanting to carve out a new purpose, to find yourself, to push on when you are lacking a support group or when you feel alone.

In today's uncertain climate, living with purpose has never been more important.

The world is different. From our political landscape to the shaky economy to the fallout from the COVID-19 pandemic, the "meaning" of life might look significantly different than it ever has before.

Maybe you lost a family member to the virus. Maybe you lost your job. Maybe you feel like you lost your purpose and are grappling with how to find your way back to a new normal.

At times you're optimistic, but most likely, you're also scared, stressed, and even pissed. You may be fearful of the future. Or uncertain about what you should do next.

Though it's easier said than done, so much of your anxiety and uncertainty comes from the focus on what you can't control: circumstances, media, and other people's fear and panic. The only thing you can do is to control what matters to you. If you control your thoughts, feelings, and actions, you can dictate how you feel, how you want to live your life, and how to lead with purpose in everything that you do.

Those are choices that are always in your control, regardless of what's happening in the world, politics, or the economy.

---

*Purpose First Entrepreneur* will help you take control of your life, maximize your potential, and create a thriving business that has a lasting impact on others.

But it starts with personal accountability. Become the leader of your life. Grab the wheel. Take ownership of your destiny. Focus on what really matters to you.

Not just when shit hits the fan.
Not just when our politicians screw up.
Not just when a school tragedy happens.
Not just when the war for racial equality flares up.
Not just when the news portrays an apocalyptic world.
Not just when you're scared, uncertain, or panicked.

It's time to be purposeful on a *regular* basis and make daily decisions that lead to optimal performance, success, and satisfaction—in your business, at home, and everywhere in between.

***

This book will show you how to find purpose in your work, capitalize on that purpose, and use it to manifest dreams, success, and measurable outcomes that you can continue to apply in your day-to-day actions. To make a greater impact, you have to show up every single day. (This is not like last year's New Year's resolution that faded into oblivion after a few weeks. This is about real, effective change.)

I've spent more than a decade cracking the code around the mind-boggling complexity of achieving great results and sustaining optimal performance. I've deciphered, researched, and studied human behavior and performance to figure out how you can improve your performance as an entrepreneur. How can you get more wins and experience fewer failures?

Before you get to all that, however, you have to *define* purpose, or rather, purposeful living.

Purposeful living is driven by your values, your beliefs, and what matters to you. Purposeful living allows us to be our best—a best that is not defined by our employers, partners, or government.

Our best is defined by us.

Because here's the thing—while you have good intentions to succeed, to do your very best, to live an intentional life, you often let fear, loss, anger, hate, uncertainty, ego, and even pain dictate reality.

You forget that you can lead your own life.
You forget that you have an innate purpose unique to you.
You forget that what you do can—and should—be aligned with your purpose.

At the end of the day, are you going to let your life become one big participation trophy? Do you want a meaningless token for just being here? Or are you going to feel satisfied knowing you did what you were put on this planet to do?

No matter what category you fall into, you will learn to own and maximize your own sense of purpose to create greater value for yourself, the businesses you lead, and the world you inhabit. As a bonus, if you want to go deeper on any of these Purpose First principles, please visit PurposeFirstEntrepreneur.com/workbook to download the companion workbook as you read.

While *Purpose First Entrepreneur* can't tell you how to live your life, it creates the framework for a new way to think so that you can make good decisions appropriate to the circumstances of your life and your business, as well as how you think, feel, and perform on a daily basis.

Once you have your purpose defined, honed, and optimized, you no longer have to ask: *What is my purpose? What do I believe in? How do I live a life that matters?*

You'll be living and leading the way you were always meant to, regardless of the world around you. You'll have your answers. You'll stay true to the path.

This *knowing* is what you will explore here, one principle at a time.

# CHAPTER 1

# WHAT DO YOU DO?

How many times have you asked someone, "What do you do?" They respond, you tune out, and then you move on to other topics. Maybe their job isn't that interesting, or maybe they don't sound excited when they talk about it.

So often, we equate *who we are* with *what we do* ... but so many of us don't like what we do. We use our careers as a means to an end. It's a paycheck! It's got great benefits! It's the responsible path!

But what if there were a way to marry your life's purpose *with* the work you do? To feel engaged, excited, and driven by meaning every single day? To start a business that will change the world?

After I was violently attacked, I believed that anything could be taken from me at any moment for no reason, which was a pretty lousy feeling. I didn't think I'd ever feel engaged, excited, or driven by meaning again.

I decided that even though I couldn't control the outside world, I didn't want to feel helpless. So I made a decision. I wanted to lead my life my way.

I didn't make some grandiose promise to myself that everything was going to change overnight. I made a simple decision to focus my attention on what I could control and forget about what I couldn't.

And a moment was all I really needed.

Focusing on the present helped me stabilize. It also prevented me from dwelling on what was "supposed" to happen in the future. While I worked on my mind, I watched my body change. I went from playing college football at a fit 200 pounds to being an emaciated 145-pound teenager who could barely walk in a straight line.

My head was shaved, with stitches traversing from the front to the back like a zipper. I lost my short-term memory, had difficulty hearing people speak, and wasn't able to talk in full sentences. So, needless to say, I would often envision the rest of my life in a pretty shitty state.

But I decided to become present and mindful before I even knew what those terms meant, because it was all I *could* do. It was the only control I possessed. Whenever my thoughts about the future became fearful, I would tell myself, *You're safe now. You have control of what matters.* I would then clear my mind and focus only on the moment, what I was doing, and how I was feeling.

Correction—how I *wanted* to feel.

Over time, I continued to return to one question a lot: *Am I safe?* When thoughts about being physically and mentally limited for the rest of my life would consume my mind, I would tell myself, *I'm doing what the doctors and rehab professionals told me to, so I'm doing the best I can.*

I decided to only address any long-term issues once they became a reality, not when they were just the gnawing fears in my head. I didn't have the energy to create an idea of what things *could* be like. I only had the capacity to focus on what I wanted to *feel* like. What I would feel like, in time.

I now know if I hadn't focused on staying in the moment, I wouldn't have survived.

I also knew I needed hope. I needed purpose. Nothing huge (according to many people's standards), but I needed something to provide some direction in my life. For me, that was going back to college and getting my business degree. This provided clarity, intentionality, and a concrete goal. (And clearly, I was very motivated because I was paying for college myself.) Along the way, I started to rebuild myself and physically heal. I was also fortunate to have family and friends support me in healing my emotional scars.

As I healed, I became more aware of the opportunities in life. I could have become bitter because life wasn't treating me the way it was treating others. However, I flipped it around. I could have been dead, but I'd received a second chance. I was going to make the best of it, however I could. I quickly learned that while life wasn't turning out the way I thought it would, it was laying the foundation for an entirely new way of being.

Once my quest for purpose emerged, I began to feel like I was *more* than my experiences. There was more than death, grief, and loss. I was more than fear or uncertainty. I just had to find it. After overcoming so many of life's hurdles, I was able to look at life in a new way. I began asking myself:

*What is my calling?*
*How can I make a difference in the world?*
*What is my purpose?*

For most of us, this can mean more than one thing. You will have to discover it for yourself.

For me, it was becoming an entrepreneur. Although I didn't realize it at the time, it's clear now. Entrepreneurs think *big*. We believe we can change the world. We see things that no one else sees and create ideas, concepts, businesses, and products from scratch. We provide meaning and give people purpose to make the world a better place, regardless of whether it's a new widget or the cure for a rare disease. Entrepreneurs provide purpose to their teams and give them the opportunity to do something no one has ever done before.

My life as an entrepreneur and venture investor has reinforced the importance of purpose. Purpose provides clarity, attentiveness, and motivation to achieve and experience the things that matter most in life. Your purpose might be something simple or something big. Regardless, this book will help you discover it and manifest it within your start-up.

We are wired to seek more, crave more, have more, and do more, right? But if you slow down and get honest with yourself about your purpose and your life, what do you really want? What do you really crave?

My life experience provided unique insights into the pursuit of purpose and a meaningful life, but so have my work experiences. Before I was thirty, I was a critical part of two technology start-ups that sold and IPO-ed for more than $2.8 billion. I later went on to lead the turnaround of a medical education company from record losses to record profits, which I followed by starting a double-bottom-line company focused on college attainment for Latino families. Not every step was successful, but they were all purposeful.

Today, I am an active venture investor. I lead one of the most active and successful early-stage investor groups in the country. We have partnered with hundreds of founders to help turn their dreams into reality, helping them scale their businesses from start-up ideas to global market leaders. As a result, we have created billions of dollars of value, but more importantly, we helped these founders manifest their purposes into incredible companies that are changing the world.

In addition to my own personal and professional experience with the power of purpose, I needed more evidence, both qualitative and quantitative, to truly understand it in a pragmatic and philosophical way. I studied, researched, explored, experimented, and documented. I dug into scientific data, tested a variety of apps, studied a spectrum of religions, analyzed the lives of historical leaders, and quantified every key aspect of my life for nearly a decade. I wanted to develop a theory that would be applicable to everyone, in all situations. Something that would

# CHAPTER 2

# HOW TO DISCOVER YOUR PURPOSE

What is the meaning of your life?

Why do some people know what they want and have an intoxicating zest for life and others languish in confusion, feeling lost and unfulfilled?

Purpose provides the key to unlocking your true potential. You are more. There is more! But you have to have purpose to get there.

Entrepreneurs are the quintessential example of living with purpose. They consciously or subconsciously discover their life's purpose. Despite the known risks associated with the endeavor, they relentlessly pursue turning their passions into reality for the benefit of others. Their quests to fulfill their destinies empower them to snap the mental chains that hold them back. Purpose infuses them with the resilience needed to overcome whatever obstacles they encounter along the way.

Everyone is an entrepreneur in a way. People are seeking to discover their unique purpose and manifest it by building something great in their lives. However, unlike an entrepreneur, most manifest their purpose outside of founding a start-up.

While the majority of us realize we're here for a specific reason, it's often hard to pinpoint exactly what that reason is, or how to hold on to it when shit hits the fan (which, as we've all just experienced with the pandemic, it does).

I like to think of purpose as the *opposite* of kryptonite. Instead of a force that destroys superheroes, it turns ordinary people into extraordinary humans. Unfortunately, it doesn't come in the form of a rock, potion, or pill. You have to find it for yourself.

Sometimes it finds you. It finds you when you see an injustice, when you lose a loved one to an incurable disease, when you see someone do something incredible, when you create a solution to a problem that no one else can solve, when you share a talent that makes other people feel better.

Purpose is like that one friend who always has your back. You know, the one who doesn't mind if your shoes don't match your belt, if you're not looking your best, or if you have green, leafy spinach lodged in your teeth. Purpose puts her hand out and helps your sorry butt up when you fall, getting you back to your feet to go at it again. Purpose will help you battle cancer, recover from addiction, and heal your heart.

Purpose helps you live.

Once you've got it—and I mean *really* got it—you walk the walk, talk the talk, and fight the fight. You let go of the crazy scramble to figure out what you're supposed to be doing with your life, because *now you know*. Once you know, it grows more powerful. It gets stronger. It becomes a multiplier. And before you know it, other people have it too (thanks to your awesome example).

So how the hell do you find it? Or, if you find it, what are you supposed to do with it? That's what we're going to uncover together.

# FIND YOUR PURPOSE

Throughout history, countless people have identified their purpose. (You know who they are.) Though most of us will not ever be remembered as well as Mother Teresa or have the same impact as Nelson Mandela, viewing others' purposes can sometimes help clarify our own. Think about Steve Jobs, Arianna Huffington, Bill Gates, Tina Fey, LeBron James, Abe Lincoln, Oprah, and even that mountain climber who lives out of his van (yes, even he has a purpose).

Somehow, these wildly successful individuals managed to identify their purpose, capitalize on it, and then share it with the world.

The good news? You're next.

Here are some facts: you possess all the value you will ever have. You will never become more valuable or worthy than this moment. That self-worth and self-value are inherent. You are worth something. That is a fact. Humanity is worth something. But if you don't identify your purpose *within* your value, and how it relates to your family, your partner, your kids, your team, your community, or even the world, then chances are, nothing you want will materialize.

Many of us don't know where we want to go or are reevaluating our original view of where we thought we wanted to be. That's ok. Our lives evolve. We have new experiences, new data points to calibrate our lives and point them in the right direction.

If you want to live your best life, you must view yourself as the leader of it. Good leaders create an inspiring vision of the future, develop a plan to realize the vision, and oversee the successful execution of the plan. Therefore, as the leader of your life and an aspiring Purpose First Entrepreneur, you are responsible for creating a vision of yourself centered around purpose.

❶ **ATTENTION, PLEASE:** Go to PurposeFirstEntrepreneur.com/workbook to download your companion workbook. It is a great resource to help you organize your thoughts, translate them into actions, and turn those actions into a thriving business and life.

## THREE PURPOSE QUESTIONS

We will start by answering the **Three Purpose Questions** to help
you discover your purpose:

**Purpose**

1. What do you love to do?

2. What are your strengths?

3. How will you make the world better?

It sounds easy, right? Answer some questions and ta-da!
Purposeful living at your fingertips! Not so fast. While so many of
us want to live a life of purpose, so few of us give any real time
or attention to thinking purposefully. We go around and around
with the same set of thoughts, which results in the same outcomes.
The same complaints. The same setbacks. Now it's finally time to
take control of your life.

## WHAT DO YOU LOVE TO DO?

Let's attempt to uncover the meaning of your life. What do you live
for? What are you willing to die for? What do you need to do to
live your best life? These questions are powerful. They really make
us probe deep down, beneath the surface, where it really matters.
They help us explore the purpose of our lives and establish the
truth we live by.

If you feel unsatisfied with your life, frustrated with your
job, or empty inside, you are likely seeking meaning in your life.
Discovering your purpose and manifesting it in your life will help

on in college and eventually earned a scholarship—I just wasn't going to make it to the NFL.

Identifying your strengths is a critical part of realizing your purpose. Aligning your passions with your natural talents significantly enhances the probability that you will be successful. If your passion doesn't align with your abilities, it doesn't mean you have to give up. You can pursue a different path that aligns your skills with your passions. For example, I could have played football as long as my abilities allowed me to, then pursued a coaching career instead of playing football.

That may be the same case for many entrepreneurs. They can start the company, get it to a great place, but need to hand it off at some point to a person with a different skill set for operationalizing companies. The person you hand it off to wouldn't be able to do what you did either. You know, build something from scratch and turn it into a rapidly growing business. Neither person is better. Each has different skill sets and circumstances to allow them to perform at their best.

Your *abilities* provide a baseline for the work needed to reach your goals. You can benchmark them against the general population for context. You can also compare them to elite performers in your field to get more granular. You can benchmark improvements in or degradation of your abilities against your own performance over time. Nevertheless, understanding what you do well and what you do poorly will help you make important decisions in life.

You have a core decision to make: (1) build on your strengths or (2) strengthen your weaknesses. If you build on your strengths, you will need external support to address the areas where you are weak. However, if you are doing what you are strong at, gifted at—something that comes naturally—it will be easier for you to reach your desired outcome.

For example, perhaps you are great at product development but suck at coding. Should you focus on becoming an elite product visionary who is competent at coding? Or would it be better for

- How will it help?
- Why does it make the world better?

Think about the problems you will solve. The value you will create. The support you will provide. The stress you will eliminate. The joy you will instill. The people you will help. The jobs you will create. Those are just a few examples to get you thinking.

*Sure*, you say. *That's easy if you're in healthcare or education. What if I'm in accounting, for example? How does accounting change the world?* Well, it does. Without accounting professionals, everyone would be forced to do accounting. Ugh!!! However, more seriously, let me show you an example.

If you start your own accounting firm specializing in creative freelance professionals, you will help your clients get the best financial and tax solutions for their specific needs. It will take the accounting burden off these freelance professionals, allowing them to operate their businesses more profitably and focus more time on their creative work. Thus, you are doing what you love to do and do well while empowering your clients to fill the world with inspiration and creativity. Thus, you and your clients are making the world better in your own unique ways.

It doesn't matter whether your business simplifies a single, mundane task or produces a game-changing technology; every business has an opportunity to improve the world. By sharing your talent and passion with those who need it, you make the world better.

I recommend writing down your answers to each of the questions in a notebook or in the Purpose First Entrepreneur workbook. Don't spend a lot of time justifying the answers. That's a mistake. You'll likely get caught up in self-imposed skepticism. Don't doubt yourself. This exercise is all about you as your best self. You are capable of great things. You are rewriting your life. Anything is possible!

To help with the process, consciously tap into your inner strength and the powerful emotions that motivate you to dream big. You may even want to listen to your favorite motivational podcast. Watch your favorite inspirational movie. Or read an autobiography about someone you admire. Often these legendary figures are ordinary folks, just like you, who made an extraordinary impact on the world. They struggled with their own self-doubt, insecurities, and demons while battling a variety of external forces that prevented them from achieving their dreams. However, they triumphed in the end and fulfilled their destinies.

The common denominator between these luminaries is they all had big purpose. It was a driving force that propelled them to success. It gave their lives meaning and made an impact on the world well beyond anything they could have dreamed.

## DEVELOP YOUR PURPOSE VISION

*Purpose First Entrepreneur* will help you manifest your purpose into a business you love and provide the meaning in life you are seeking. So let's turn the abstract idea of purpose into reality.

The first step is refining your purpose. Go back and review your answers to the Three Purpose Questions, which were designed to identify your purpose. Think about how they make you feel. Yep. Really allow yourself an opportunity to feel. If you drink, you may know the feeling. After you've had one too many, your mind may not be guarding your feelings and rationalizing your dreams. You start to talk about how you are going to quit your job and move on to something bigger and better. It's the feelings associated with daydreaming about following your heart. About being your best, enjoying what you're doing, and having a big impact on the world. How would that make you feel?

Make sure your answers capture that—but without the booze. Jot down the key elements that emerge for each question. Evaluate them. Which matters more? Matters less? You can even stack rank them in a list to help home in on what really matters to you. When you're done with this step, you should have identified and prioritized (1) what you love to do, (2) what you are good at, and (3) how it will make the world better.

The next step is to share your answers with the important people in your life. This may be tough because you are sharing your deepest hopes, beliefs, and dreams. Many have learned in life that sharing this sensitive and private information can backfire. You may believe that in sharing this, you'll put yourself at risk for being hurt. At the same time, you may also have experienced how empowering it is to have these hopes and dreams validated and supported. It empowers you to make them a reality. So do it! It may even help you take your purpose to the next level.

Now. You've identified your purpose. The type of purpose that will get you out of bed, help you kick some butt, and turn you into a superhero of perseverance. Let's make it a part of your life! Let's capture the essential elements of your answers and create your Purpose Vision.

Your **Purpose Vision** is essential. It allows you to get your true north for your life. It is similar to a compass; your Purpose Vision will orient you to where you want to go, regardless of how lost you may seem at times. It will create a beacon for your life. How to be your best self and have the biggest impact on the world.

You must be able to visualize yourself different than you are now. You have to see yourself realizing your purpose. You need to connect with the feelings that are associated with the experience. Envision the impact you have on the world and the tremendous value it has created for you and others. Imagine the emotions that will be triggered, knowing you made a big difference in making the world better.

Your Purpose Vision will describe how you will manifest your purpose into a thriving business to improve the world. See the example below:

*As the founder of an internationally recognized blockchain start-up, I'm transforming how people's integrity can be shifted from financial capital to social capital (their honor) to secure loans and create wealth. My team and I created a new system to reward and empower people everywhere, regardless of race, gender, religion, and socioeconomic status. We will make a positive impact on peoples' lives throughout the world, thus inspiring us to lead our best lives.*

Now, create your own Purpose Vision. Be sure to include your role in making your vision a reality. It will help you envision your future self. Push outside your comfort zone about what you are truly capable of achieving with your business. Feel free to incorporate others into your vision and consider how those relationships inspire you to do great things for the people you serve. Infuse language about what you will accomplish, experience, or feel. Be sure to weave in how leading with purpose has a meaningful impact on your life.

Turn your vision into a plan. Immediately. If you write it down in your workbook, you will increase your success rate. Don't overthink it. Establish long-term and short-term goals based on your Purpose Vision. What are your objectives for where you want to be in five years? What objectives do you need to accomplish in the next year to get to that five-year goal? For example, you know, at the very least, you want to be running a successful business in five years. Write that down. You also know that you need a business plan to start that business this year. Your goals can be qualitative or quantitative. Whatever works for you. I recommend establishing SMART (Specific, Measurable, Attainable, Relevant, and Timely) goals, but don't sweat it. Just write them down.

Next, create micro-goals. List what you need to do this week and this month to start the process. For example, your goal might be to read this book by the end of the week and come up with three ideas for your business by the end of the month. At this point, you just want to have them captured in some way. Keep in mind, we get deeper into goals, strategies, and planning later in the book. This is just an important starting point.

It's exciting to identify your purpose. You created your Purpose Vision and goals. Your adrenaline begins to pump. You start to connect. You can see yourself living with purpose, in alignment with one or more of the answers from the Three Purpose Questions.

Unfortunately, that excitement often starts to wane before we take action, and then doubt starts to creep in. All of those voices telling us why we can't do it. Or the fact that we are trained—no, conditioned—to stay in our comfortable little bubbles. Biologically, when we stay in our comfort zones, we are safe. While this literally used to mean the difference between life or death, now it means the difference between having a safe life or a purposeful one. We certainly don't want to push beyond what everyone else is doing, right? I mean, if you try and you fail, you are a *failure*, right? So it's better not to try.

Except it's not.

I'll let you in on a little secret: everyone fails. *Everyone.* The billionaire start-up founder, the high-profile VC investor, the entrepreneur who you think has all the answers … every single human fails. It's what you *do* with that failure and how you turn it into action that matters.

If you've only failed once, that's not enough. Failing once doesn't really show you what you're made of or what to learn. What we want to explore here is *optimal* failure. (That's right, you can ensure you fail the right way. Who knew?) Right now, you might be *sub*optimal because you don't take enough risk. You have to get out of your comfort zone in order for failure to become an option. If you try, fail, then give up, what did you really learn?

However, if you fail five times around the same idea, is that better? No. Failing five times trying the same thing is too much because you're not recognizing the *pattern* of your failure well enough to appropriately course-correct; hence, the failure is suboptimal because you are not producing the necessary results.

So how do you reach optimal failure?

expect someone else to solve their problems. They might complain that the government, their company, a business, or boss put them in their situation. But at the end of the day, it doesn't matter whose fault it is—only *you* can take ownership of your life.

As you do that, people who don't will feel threatened and look to bring you down. Not everyone will act this way, but those who do (especially close friends and family) will make you doubt what you're doing. Once people start to notice you are taking a different route, they might say, *"Hey, what is so special about you? Get back in line. Be average. Be like us. We don't like it. You are making us uncomfortable for not trying."*

When that happens—and it will—do not listen. Live your purpose. Hold your ground. Be strong. Just like MLK, who was in a career that he loved. It wasn't a job; it was his life. Find something that you love and you are good at. If you don't have the luxury of founding a start-up or being a part of a company that fits those criteria, look outside of your job. However, find something that's aligned with your purpose. Use your job as the work you do in order to do the things you love.

By doing this, you can uncover your very best self.

Revisit your Purpose Vision often. See it. Picture yourself living your life as your best self. Like you were given a magic wand and could make anything happen. What will your life look like? How will you feel? How will others feel? Will you give them all their own magic wands too? (Just go with it. Wands are super cool.)

Remember: if you live purposefully, you will inspire others to live a purposeful life too.

Inspiring others is powerful. It's contagious. Furthermore, it will push you to do more in your business, at home, and everywhere in between. It will align with the good in the universe, so more goodwill will flow.

The bottom line? A purposeful life has value. Value drives behavior. You make decisions to *act* based on the value *to you.* Whether it's consciously or subconsciously, you are assessing value all the time.

# KNOW WHAT YOU VALUE

For instance, maybe every morning when your alarm goes off, you press snooze. You get a few extra minutes of sleep, but you are rushing around like a chicken with its head cut off to get to work on time. You do it *every single day.* Whether you realize it or not, you made a conscious decision that the comfort of your bed is more *valuable* than the annoyances of rushing around in an anxiety-riddled stupor every morning. Sleep has more value than the coffee you spill, the boss you piss off, or the spouse you annoy.

You have trained your mind to make this chaotic routine part of your daily life. Take a moment and examine all the things or practices you might have accidentally given your value to. Is it your phone, where you spend endless hours consuming conflicting information instead of paying attention to your child? Is it yelling in traffic instead of using that time to unwind or assess your day? Is it numbing yourself with Netflix and a drink instead of tuning in to your family or yourself? Is it spending ten hours per day at a job you hate instead of figuring out what business you actually want to start and making it happen?

Where does your value truly go on a daily basis? What have you allowed to become your "normal"?

Make sure that your choices—your purposes—line up with what you really value. You have to make purposeful decisions. Decisions control your life. Yep, your decisions are critical to manifesting the life you want. So own them. (We will spend a lot more time on this in upcoming chapters.)

# A PURPOSE FIRST CASE STUDY

I work with a lot of entrepreneurs as an early-stage investor. Many entrepreneurs are so confident in their purpose, they act. They don't overthink or consider alternatives. They quit their jobs or course-correct and commit themselves to making their purpose a reality.

They decide to be bold.

Usually, by the time I talk to an entrepreneur, they have started the company and have customers or users of some sort. They are telling me how people love the product, how the market for their product is huge, and how the big companies are too slow to make a shift. We talk about metrics, numbers, and other VC stuff. But what I will really love is the enthusiasm. I can feel that they believe in themselves.

Many times entrepreneurs are extremely passionate about a problem because they are experiencing it themselves and assume others are in the same boat.

For example, an entrepreneur I know, Katlin Smith, fits the bill perfectly. She'd suffered from joint pain and a poor diet for a long time, which affected every other aspect of her life. To make a long story short, Katlin took a hard look at her eating habits and opted for more whole, natural foods. She soon discovered a lack of options for prepared food—especially baked goods—without chemicals or additives.

Her own experience made her think. She believed if she created a company to solve this problem, it would change people's lives. It would give them something they desperately wanted—a natural baking mix that was free of gluten, grains, soy, and genetically modified ingredients. She predicted that people would stop buying the baking mixes they'd bought for years and buy her products.

Well, Katlin was right.

Today, Simple Mills—the number-one clean-label baking mix and cracker brand and number-three cookie brand in the natural channel—is a driving force in transforming the center grocery aisles with innovative whole-food snack alternatives in categories traditionally lacking better-for-you options. The company's products are distributed in tens of thousands of stores, including Whole Foods, Kroger, Publix, Safeway, and Target.

As Winston Song, managing director of Vestar, a leader in

consumer product goods investing, explains, "Simple Mills has helped shape the next generation natural food movement, fundamentally changing consumers' concepts of healthy food."[1]

Katlin's passion became a company, a brand promise, and a reality.

How can you be like Katlin? Sometimes, our setbacks can lead us to problem-solve, to create a solution in our own lives that can then translate to others.

Let's dig a little deeper into your purpose.

# CHAPTER 3

# YOUR PURPOSE PILLARS, EXPLAINED

I explained the importance of purpose in living your life with meaning. It will help you build a successful business and live according to what is important to you. But what if I told you that there's something even more important than your purpose for directing your life and achieving your goals? I know, you're probably like, "WTF, Pete, after everything you hammered home in the last chapter, what could be more important than my purpose?" But hear me out on this.

Don't get me wrong, having purpose is a major catalyst for making your start-up idea a reality. A strong vision of the life you want to live turns possibilities into reality. However, to help you realize your goals, you need a strong foundation on which to build your success. Something that keeps it all in check. Enter your **Purpose Pillars**: Honor, Love, Wellness, and Goodness.

Purpose Pillars strengthen your purpose by anchoring it to the core principles of your life. These Pillars represent the essential elements you must build and maintain to be your best. *Honor, love, wellness,* and *goodness* mean different things to different people.

## Purpose Pillars

Therefore, you have to personalize each Pillar for you. It's up to you to define each Pillar, and it's your job to keep them strong. Living according to your Purpose Pillars is critical for long-term personal satisfaction—even more so than achieving extraordinary accomplishments like taking your start-up public.

"Why?" you might ask.

Think of it this way: you either reach that one big goal, or you fail to reach it. Either way, the euphoria or sadness eventually fades away. And just like that, it's in the past. Now what do you have left? If you have maintained your Purpose Pillars along the way, you have the foundation for a wonderful life. They create a lot more meaning for your life beyond accomplishing your goals. They propel you to live every day according to your principles, allowing you to become the best version of yourself.

Purpose Pillars establish the personal and professional code you live by. They lay the foundation for how you operate. When a founder doesn't have clear Purpose Pillars, their business won't either. Your company's culture will tell you what type of leader you are and the values you have. So don't wait! Tune in to what you stand for and build some incredible Purpose Pillars for yourself and your company.

There are four Purpose Pillars: Honor, Love, Wellness, and Goodness. I will provide a framework for you to discover what each means to you and how they translate to your business. If you believe you need to add other Pillars that are unique to you, I encourage you to do so since this exercise is deeply personal. They will help you set the standards you live by, guiding your behavior in your business and life.

> ❶ **ATTENTION, PLEASE:** The companion workbook will help you create your Purpose Pillars. Visit PurposeFirstEntrepreneur.com/workbook.

## PURPOSE PILLARS

# HONOR

Many people don't truly know *their* core values. We are heavily influenced by others in what we think, feel, and believe (sometimes unknowingly so). So many of our beliefs are unconsciously adopted from our culture, society, and media. If you strip everything away, what are your core values? It's easy to regurgitate what others say you should value. But knowing your truth and practicing it takes effort.

The Purpose Pillar of **Honor** helps you define what you stand for. Or better stated, it's your *personal code of honor*. It defines your truth and how to apply it to your life, regardless of the circumstances. It also helps avoid the empty feelings that emerge when you are incongruent with your values. Furthermore, as a Purpose First Entrepreneur, this Pillar will help you infuse honor it into the culture of your company.

Let's create your personal code of honor. First, reflect on your values. Make a list of them. Identify what matters to you at work and in life. What are your core beliefs? What are nonnegotiables? What do you honor? The table below provides a list of values that you may consider. It is not meant to be an all-inclusive list but a primer to get you thinking, so feel free to add your own. You may include values that have influenced you over time. They may have emerged from a variety of sources including religion, family, friends, teams, etc. Outside influences often shape your thinking, beliefs, and values. However, before you add any to your list, be sure they represent you. Make sure you undoubtedly believe and will relentlessly honor them, regardless of the circumstances.

## Values

| | |
|---|---|
| Accountable | Honest |
| Authentic | Independent |
| Autonomous | Integrity |
| Collaborative | Just |
| Compassionate | Loyal |
| Courageous | Loving |
| Curious | Perseverant |
| Dedicated to Doing Your Best | Resilient |
| Dependable | Respectful |
| Determined | Responsible |
| Dignified | Self-Respectful |
| Empathic | Selfless |
| Equitable | Spiritual |
| Ethical | Successful |
| Committed to Excellence | Team Focused |
| Fair | Trustworthy |
| Free | Truthful |
| Hardworking | Wise |

After you have completed your list of values, organize them into categories. This will make your values list much more manageable and increase the likelihood you will apply them in your life. For example, I grouped several of the values under one value category, *Integrity*. To provide context, I believe in order to live with integrity, you have to be *accountable, authentic, dependable, ethical, honest, responsible,* and *truthful.* The meaning of each value may be different for you, so you can create your own categories. However, you want to narrow your list. Ideally, you will have three to five values categories. Too many and you'll have difficulty adhering to them.

Once you have your values aligned, encapsulate them in a single statement. For example, here is my Pillar of Honor statement: *I am committed to leading my life with Honor by treating others and myself with Respect, acting with Integrity, and always Doing My Best.*

My honor code is straightforward. It has three value categories: Respect, Integrity and Doing My Best. Not only have these values guided me, but I have also been able to pass them on to my children from an early age because they are simple yet powerful. In my family, we often referred to them by the acronym RID. And, like kids will do, we have often had fun with them. After imparting some family wisdom to my sons about the importance of one or more of the values, they have been known to joke, "We got to get rid of the RID." Although they joke about them, these values have been infused into their lives to help them to make ethical decisions. My son even wrote his college essay about the life lessons he learned from RID. I don't claim to be the father of the year, but I am proud knowing that I help establish a code of honor for my children.

Let me share insights about my honor code to help you develop yours. *Respect* is as much about respecting myself as it is respecting others. I must treat my mind, body, and emotions with respect. They are not to be undervalued or disrespected. If I can't treat myself with respect, I know I will have difficulty truly respecting others. However, if I do respect myself, I must respect others in the same way. We are all the same. No one above or below, all equals. People may lose our respect as a result of how they behave, but we must start with respect.

Like respect, *Integrity* starts with me. It is about keeping my word. Making a commitment to myself and holding myself accountable for my decisions and actions is the root of my honor code. I am responsible to myself and others. If I give my word to you, I will honor my word. If I don't agree, I am sincere, yet respectful, about my opposition. Although I may not be liked because I don't agree with a position, I will stand in my truth. Living according to my truth is more important than being liked. I hope I am liked, but I will not sacrifice my integrity to achieve it. I believe that by acting with integrity, I will earn trust from others. Once trust is earned, it forms the bond that strong relationships need to last.

The final master value in my code of honor is to *Do My Best*. Although I love to win, if I can truthfully tell myself that I have done my best, then I am satisfied, even if I don't win. This value is applied to big and little things in my life, from mundane tasks to starting a business. By living according to it, I create a framework for living well. I build muscle memory to automatically apply it in every aspect of my life. Knowing I did my best allows me to feel satisfied, regardless of the outcome. If I haven't done my best, I have failed, even if the outcome is a success. Not doing your best, cruising by, is wasteful, and it slowly erodes your potential because you have lowered the bar for what you expect of yourself, which directly impacts what you can achieve. Please keep in mind, doing my best doesn't mean being perfect. Perfect can be the enemy of progress. And progress may be the desired outcome. However, by pushing yourself to do your best to achieve your desired outcome, you will succeed, even if you fail. You know you held nothing back, which is the only metric you can really use to evaluate yourself.

Now, it is your turn. Stand up Honor as your first Purpose Pillar. Develop your code of honor. Apply it to your life. Infuse it into your business.

# LOVE

**Love** is an essential Pillar to live a happy life. It is a powerful emotion that helps us feel whole. It is a powerful connection to someone or something that makes life much fuller. Your love of your family, friends, and spiritual being are examples. Love for pets, nature, knowledge, and so much more drives deep meaning in our lives. Keep in mind, I am not referring to a romantic love. I am referring to it as a principle in your life.

Love is a principle to live by. When you say, "I live with love," it takes on a different meaning. It's a statement on your approach to how you live and how you lead your business. It becomes one of the most powerful forces to propel your start-up and life. It fosters acts of kindness, compassion, caring, and other noble actions. It helps you forgive, be patient, and act with humility. It becomes a part of your life and generates incredible satisfaction.

Being connected with love has never been more important than in our high-tech, disconnected society. Making a conscious decision to live with love profoundly changes you and the world. It helps you build a strong relationship with yourself, foster healthy relationships with others, and bring a new kind of meaning to your life.

Determine how you live with love. Make a list. This will likely complement your honor code. An easy way to get started is to determine what makes you feel loved. Is it when you are heard, supported, and treated compassionately? Start there. Then think about how you behave when you want to show love. Are you empathic, caring, and helpful? Dig in. Are there new ways you represent how you live with love? Do you need to be more patient or more accepting? Do you need to do more in service of others?

Then, write out a statement that defines this Pillar for you. For example, *I love. I love my family and friends. I live with love by helping those who I can help with my unique talents. I show empathy, demonstrate grace, and patiently help others to be their best selves. I understand I must love myself before I can fully love others. Therefore, I show myself the same compassion and kindness that I show those around me. Together, we will fill the world with love.*

Next, take inventory of who you love. What? Yep, make a list. This will help you recognize where you have joy in your life. More importantly, it provides a list of the relationships you need to make a priority. At times, you may get caught up in your start-up and put everyone you love on the back burner. However, if you don't spend any time nurturing these relationships, they will grow weaker. Before you know it, they will be gone. The energy they once provided to you turns into a bottomless pit of regret. You need to nurture them to ensure they are healthy. The stronger those relationships are, the stronger you will be, the easier it will be to live with love.

Living with Love as a Purpose Pillar in your life will make your life much richer and your business much stronger.

# WELLNESS

Your **Wellness** Pillar focuses on your physical, mental, and emotional well-being. You are more likely to realize your Purpose Vision and achieve your goals if you take care of yourself. As an entrepreneur, your physical, mental, and emotional health is critical. Your ability to make good decisions directly correlates with your health. Making wellness a priority improves your life and your employees' lives. Healthy people perform better and build better businesses.

Despite all the evidence, many entrepreneurs dismiss the importance of self-care and brag about their relentless grind. However, this is foolish and not supported by science.

Fortunately, the basics of wellness are not complicated. We have long known about living well—get enough sleep, eat right, and exercise. However, we all know you must be committed, which is why wellness needs to be a Purpose Pillar in your life. We must commit to our wellness by making it our lifestyle. A few seamless ways to do so are making it a part of your daily routine and incorporating it into the culture of the business you lead.

Being aware of mental and emotional well-being is important. However, it can be complicated. A lifetime of experiences and corresponding emotions shapes us; some are feelings that serve us very well and some hold us back or down. Our demons—fears and anxieties—lurk in the shadows. We often battle our internal shadows as we seek the powerful light of our purpose. It can be exhausting. Self-exploration, meditation, spirituality, fostering loving relationships, and seeking the support of healthcare professionals can help us understand, treat, and ultimately subdue our shadows and allow us to be emotionally healthy and live well.

Self-care can start with getting enough sleep and setting aside time to mentally, emotionally, and physically recover from the grinding workload of an entrepreneur. We should also work on developing new neural pathways (the connections in our brains) to expand what we are capable of. This can include a mindfulness practice that keeps us sharp or travel to a new country, an experience that nourishes our need for adventure and exposes us to new ideas and ways of doing things. Or we could consider taking an online course, which allows us to learn new skills that we can apply to our businesses or lives. It fosters personal growth, strengthens our brains, and enhances our mental acuity.

Physical, mental, and emotional well-being are built on each other. If you are exercising, you are likely to feel better mentally and emotionally. If you are feeling emotionally healthy and mentally sharp, you are more likely to get that fitness class in. If you just got done meditating or praying, you are more likely to be present in the conversation with your spouse, which as a result, will facilitate the emotional connection you needed. We really dig into mindfulness and wellness later in the book.

Wellness is an important Purpose Pillar for you to live your best life. It will also take your business to the next level if you make employee wellness a cornerstone of your company.

# GOODNESS

This Pillar focuses on something bigger than yourself—making the world a better place to live. Each one of us has a role to play. What is yours? How will your business improve the world? These are important questions to answer. No matter the size of the contribution, knowing you are making a difference will drive you, satisfy you, and increase your chances of success.

Although you are likely helping others in a variety of different ways, you have made a new powerful decision that only a very few people make—becoming a Purpose First Entrepreneur, one who leads with purpose and values. BTW, congratulations!

Purpose First Entrepreneurs contribute to the world by manifesting their purposes into businesses. This is an example of doing good in itself. Founders accept this challenge to maximize their talents and abilities and turn nothing into something. Take great artists, for example. If they never painted pictures for others to enjoy, they would be wasting their talents and robbing the world of enjoying what they are capable of creating. Purpose First Entrepreneurs do the same thing with their businesses. They create value for others to enjoy by building those businesses.

Some entrepreneurs may cure cancer while others may make new types of plastics. Both make an impact. For example, without the newly formulated plastic, the cancer start-up would never have been able to design and manufacture their new state-of-the-art device to treat cancer. Both companies have a role in saving people's lives. They also both have a big role in creating jobs, empowering their teams, and making the communities where they operate better.

In addition to *what* they build, Purpose First Entrepreneurs make a huge impact with *how* they build. You have the opportunity to make the world better by championing diversity, equity, and inclusiveness. Furthermore, you can help highlight and integrate the best values and attributes of your people into your company. As a result, the entire organization becomes stronger. It has a solid ethical foundation as a Purpose First Business.

Purpose First Entrepreneurs insist on working with people with strong character. Together, they build strong Purpose Pillars for the company, molding the necessary foundation to ensure the culture fosters a spirit of goodness while achieving financial and business goals. This approach creates a sustainable cycle of doing good, which all starts when an entrepreneur takes their first step in turning their Purpose Vision into a business.

Defining and living with Goodness will create a Purpose Pillar in your life, pushing you to make an impact on the world that is much bigger than yourself.

## PURPOSE PILLAR PERSPECTIVE

Your Purpose Pillars give you the foundation to achieve great things. But they also allow you to realize great things every single day by routinely doing the little things that matter to you—from living aligned with certain values to nurturing relationships that really matter to having your team volunteer in your community in order to ensure it thrives.

Failure and success will come and go, but at the end of your life, you will be the judge of how you lived. You are the only one who will truly know if it was the way you wanted. Taking accountability for your life is important. It's normal to struggle. Living a life with purpose can be hard. We all have emotional scars, human flaws, cognitive biases, and improvements to make. But if we're mindful every day about being our best, if we are putting ourselves on the field and challenging ourselves, *that's* where the joy of the journey really is. Not in the wins. Not in the results.

The joy is in living according to what is important to you.

Let's look at three different scenarios of how Purpose Pillars (or lack of) may play out in life.

1. You manifested your Purpose Vision into a business that's thriving. Then, the pandemic occurred. Your business imploded. You'd neglected everything in the singular pursuit of your business. Now you're jobless because your business had to declare bankruptcy. You're unhealthy because you ate like shit and didn't work out. And you're broke. Basically, you have nothing. If you'd had strong Pillars, you'd have a foundation for recovery. You would have had friends, family, and community to pick you up, dust you off, and get you ready to go again.

2. You achieved your goal. Your start-up succeeded. After the initial euphoria, you look around. Because you didn't pay attention to your Purpose Pillars, you find that your family is disconnected and your friends don't celebrate with you. Your true friends gave up on you, and your "new" friends enjoy your money but don't really give a damn about you. You achieved what you really wanted (or so you thought), but you feel empty. You had no foundation. Not to mention, you're prediabetic because you didn't take care of yourself.

3. You focused on nurturing your Purpose Pillars (apply to scenario 1 or 2). Although you needed to spend time to maintain them, they always made you re-energized to truly pursue your Purpose Vision. Your Pillars guided you to nurture your relationships, spend time helping others, and take care of your mind and body. They created a certain balance that allowed you to navigate the ups and downs a lot more effectively and more sustainably, so regardless of the outcome of your business, your journey and life were successful.

By grounding your life with your Purpose Pillars, you will align what matters to you at the very core of how you live. They will help you define what you do and how you do it. Although they

goal—you have to believe you can do it (or that you've already done it!), even if you aren't quite there yet. Have you ever heard of someone climbing to the peak of a mountain thinking every step of the way that they'll never get there? Heck no! They're cheering themselves on, knowing that they can reach the top. And even if they don't know it as *fact*, they still believe it.

Every year, I take a hiking trip with a group of friends. I don't particularly like heights. I get an uneasy feeling when I'm on a ladder or looking out a window of a glass elevator or climbing up a mountain. But I do it anyway.

On my first mountain hiking trip, my friends wanted to go off the trail to get to the mountain summit. We were at a high-elevation campsite. From our view, it looked pretty easy to climb up the side of the mountain to get to the peak a thousand feet or so up. However, there was no trail, and it was steep. But from where we were sitting, it didn't look too scary. Keep in mind, I don't mean steep like you need climbing gear to scale it, but steep enough that it would take you a long time to stop falling if you lost your balance, not to mention that every bone in your body would probably be broken. (However, experienced mountain climbers would laugh.)

Well, one of the four guys decided he would stay at the camp when we did this. The first five hundred feet were pretty straightforward. However, as we started our ascent, the gradient became steeper. It was much different up close (versus looking at it from afar). The guys I was with were much more adventurous than me and more comfortable with heights.

However, as we kept climbing, all of us realized that we no longer had an option to go down—up was the only way. We got to a point where it was just too steep to safely go down. At this point, my heart was racing, and I really thought I had a 50/50 chance of falling to my death.

That said, I was there. I had no option but to go up. It really made me get present and face my fear. I thought to myself, *This is really freaking scary*. And truthfully, I was pissed off at the guys I was with. Why were we even up here? Whose idea was this?

However, I knew from my life experiences that I needed to focus on my current situation. I needed to break it down into one step at a time. I wouldn't look too far ahead, because it seemed insurmountable, and I wouldn't look down, because it was really scary. I would look exactly where my foot went next. Then I would look at where my other foot went. I would make sure each foot was in a place that would allow me to maintain my balance with my hands.

I stopped focusing on why I was there and who got me there. I took control of what I could, which quite literally was one step at a time. This calmed my mind and subdued my fears—somewhat. Surprisingly, each step forward made me a little more confident. Focusing on the moment and what I could control, and forgetting about what I couldn't or why I was there, allowed me to move forward.

(Since I'm writing this, you can guess that I didn't miss a step or fall a few thousand feet to my death. Instead, I reached the top.)

When I got there, I was euphoric. Not because of the view, but because I conquered my fear the only way you can, one step at time. When things get tough, this experience is so clear in mind; I reference it all the time. I tell myself, *Take it one step at a time.* Control what you can control. You'll be really pleased when you get to the top.

In life, there is nothing that will hold you back more than yourself; training your brain to believe you can achieve greatness is what will separate you from everyone else.

I know what you're thinking—easier said than done. Why? Because many of us have developed habits shaped by cultural pressures to consistently produce average results. As if actually accomplishing those extraordinary, above-average goals is not an option for the majority. Or, even worse, we hold ourselves back because we don't want to alienate ourselves, thinking that acknowledging our greatness is conceited.

Your brain has been wired for average. In order to become elite—to become your best self—you must rewire your brain for the extraordinary.

The first step to deciding your goals is to envision your success. You can't achieve it if you don't see it—or more importantly, if you don't believe, you can't achieve it. So own this. Believe in yourself.

So what does it even mean to be a Purpose First Entrepreneur?

A Purpose First Entrepreneur is powered by her purpose to lead a business that *has* purpose. She is using her Purpose First energy to attract others—her team, clients, and partners—to unite around a unique approach, innovative solution, or new way to transform an old business and deliver a greater good.

Although many people think "Purpose First" means that the business must have a social mission, it *does not*. A Purpose First Entrepreneur is simply self-aware of her *why*, which is a part of building her Purpose Vision, which we covered in Chapter 2. By tapping into your purpose, you will be infusing innovation and opportunities into the world, which allows people to plug into, and create, something greater.

Purpose First Entrepreneurs can come in different flavors:

**Start-up Founder:** A founder is an entrepreneur who comes up with an idea and then transforms it into a business. Founders can set up a business on their own, or they can do it with others. For example, Larry Page is a founder of Google. If a founder sets up a company with other people, they are both a founder and a co-founder. So Larry Page is not only Google's founder, but also a co-founder with Sergey Brin. *Co-founder* is a term that exists to give credit to multiple people who start a business together. A co-founder may be part of the vision of a start-up from the get-go, or they may be brought on very early by the original founder because they have skills the founder is lacking. For example, the founder may have design skills but no engineering skills. In that case, it greatly benefits them to bring on a technical co-founder early in the process of launching their start-up.

**Solopreneur:** Just like the word implies, a solopreneur creates a business that only includes that person. It may be a full-time job or a side-hustle that you do when you are not at work. In addition, a lot of freelancers consider themselves solopreneurs. When this type of entrepreneur launches a business, she doesn't plan on adding full-time staff or hiring a permanent team. More and more Purpose First Entrepreneurs are choosing this path as they make a living while doing something meaningful to them such as art, fitness, teaching, writing, traveling, and a variety of other interesting pursuits.

**Business Owner:** Founders and solopreneurs own some or all of their businesses, so technically they are business owners. However, many business owners don't see themselves as entrepreneurs. They designate themselves as the owner of a repair shop, restaurant, gym, or company that falls within a spectrum of small- to medium-sized businesses. However, for this book, we consider them Purpose First Entrepreneurs.

Regardless of whether you are just starting to think about it or have been at it awhile, you are going in the right direction. By simply creating one job—even if it's your own—you have made an enormous economic difference in someone's household, the community, and the world. And by inspiring one person to think or behave more positively as a result of your business, you have made a big difference. Manifesting your purpose will ensure the world is better. This makes you a Purpose First Entrepreneur, so start your journey today.

## PURPOSE FIRST BUSINESS FUNDAMENTALS

# LAUNCH YOUR START-UP

Now it is your turn. Let me walk you through a Purpose First Entrepreneur journey. This chapter and the next will help you to start thinking about how to *start* and *fund* your **Purpose First Business**.

Let me paint a picture for you.

You love to cycle. You spend a lot of your time either cycling, learning new cycling techniques, or talking to people about cycling. You're undoubtedly passionate about cycling, which aligns with your Wellness Purpose Pillar.

The relationship with your parents and siblings has helped you become the person you are, which fits perfectly within your Love Purpose Pillar. Unfortunately, your brother has battled depression, and the stress of losing his job during the pandemic exacerbated his situation. His coping mechanisms often had him medicating himself with booze, food, and drugs. Fortunately, he got professional help. You saw him learn new skills and behaviors that allowed him to improve his emotional regulation and develop personal coping strategies that helped counter self-destructive behaviors.

To your delight, one of his new outlets was cycling. You saw how empowering it was for him. He loved it for different reasons than you did. It offered an alternative to previous negative behaviors. It allowed him to reduce his stress, gain control of what he could control, and produce dopamine (the brain's chemical reward system), which helped reinforce behaviors. It was awesome.

As exciting as it was to see your brother improve, you knew so many people in your community were struggling as a result of losing their jobs during the pandemic. Their stress levels had to be through the roof since so many had little or no savings. You wanted to help your neighbors, which ties into your Goodness Purpose Pillar. You knew many of them were going through the same thing your brother went through.

How can you help? How can you make a difference? You think about it constantly at your job as a customer success representative. You are always helping your customers get the most of the company's product. You help onboard them, teach the basics, answer questions along the way. The best part of your job is helping them. But you're also frustrated with your job. The culture is lousy, it takes a lot of energy to deal with office drama, and you don't have any ownership in the company. You yearn to align your career with your life goals. You want to be inspired and to inspire, which is why you're considering becoming a Purpose First Entrepreneur.

Here's the advice I'd give you...

# START BRAINSTORMING

Come up with a few ideas on your own. For example, (1) creating an optimal workout routine for passionate cyclists and matching them with advanced trainers, (2) developing sensors or wearables to better gauge effort and strain on an indoor bike, and (3) working with HR departments to provide a stipend for health-related activities are all ideas that connect with your Purpose Vision and Purpose Pillars.

Next, invite a few friends and colleagues to brainstorm with you on a Zoom call or over dinner. Make sure they have different strengths, abilities, and backgrounds. They should have a Purpose First Mindset *and* be talented in the areas you need the most assistance. They will help you further refine your ideas or come up with even better ones. For example, you may invite your favorite spin instructor, your friend who's in charge of product development at tech company, your partner's friend who's a software engineer, and your mom's friend who was a successful entrepreneur. If you don't have these types of personal connections, reach out to the local people or businesses match those criteria? Once you have that data, you have defined your market. Then think about whether the market is growing, shrinking, or being impacted by new trends. All of these answers will help you assess the market demand and overall business potential.

You already did some preliminary research on the impact of stress related to diabetes, anxiety, and depression and know it's a huge market. But digging deeper, you learn from the American Institute of Stress that 83% of US workers suffer from work-related stress and US businesses lose up to $300 billion a year from workplace stress. Furthermore, a million employees miss work every day due to stress-related challenges, and each year, work-related stress contributes to 120,000 deaths and $190 billion in healthcare expenses.[6]

This market research clearly aligns with your Purpose Vision and Purpose Pillars. It also validates the market size, while allowing you to further refine your initial market to focus on business professionals and employers. Narrowing your market at the beginning is very helpful in developing traction in the early stages of your business.

# BUILD AN MVP

You've validated your idea. You found the pain! Now, you would build a minimal viable product (MVP). We are going to skip the details of MVP development, which is beyond the scope of this book. There are many great resources to dive into this topic in detail; a great place to start is *The Lean Startup* by Eric Ries.

Once you have an MVP product or service in market, you are ready to start getting feedback from your users. Customer analysis is applicable regardless of whether you have a tech product or a service company or a freelance writing business. You have people (a.k.a., users, customers, clients, or whatever you want to call them) who are using what you are "selling." We need to analyze why.

# GROW THE BUSINESS

If you want to grow your business, I recommend starting with your "power users." Your power users are individuals who love your product or services. They use your solution and its features well beyond the average user. Dig into their frequency of engagement and compare it to your average users. Then you can validate it by comparing them to industry averages. You will be able to determine the percentage of your users who are power users. Although these folks will likely be around 20% of your users, they will likely make up the majority of user engagement. Understanding them is critical. They will give you the insights you need to truly grow your business. They will validate your solution and provide insights for optimizing the customer journey to build a loyal following of users while attracting new users.

You really have to be honest with yourself here. If you are not getting the data you want, do *not* fudge it. Dig in and figure out why. You will need to determine how to get enough people to use your services before you run out of money. Yep. You want to get enough users to be profitable over time. It is just a matter of how long it will take. The longer it takes, the more money (capital) you will need to raise to run your business before it is self-sustainable. Regardless, the more people using your product as power users, the better the chances you have of both becoming profitable and raising capital. We will dig into this more in the next chapter.

Your power users are going to tell you a lot. First, they will validate whether your business thesis was accurate or not. Are the

> ❶ ATTENTION, PLEASE: We are going deep in this section! You must understand your customers, their behavior, and their overall engagement (or lack thereof) with your products and services. It is mission critical for your business's long-term success. If you don't, it won't matter how purpose driven you are, you will struggle to grow your business.

people you thought were going to use your product using it? If not, who is using it? This is an important part to validate. If they are, it will help you refine your approach. Your business logic was proven correct. Now you are closer to having a product-market fit. You will have the opportunity to dig in further. Is there a way to get your power users to use more of your product, either by increasing the frequency or engaging them with new features or upgrades? You want to really understand, in their own words, why they are using it. This will help you refine your value along the customer journey.

If you create a lot of value for your power users, they will spread the word. This virality is an essential part of your business. It will turn your power users into ambassadors, spreading the word to others about the value you have created for them. This is a very key element. It is the transitive property of trust. If my friend, who I trust, tells me your product has solved her problem, and I have the same problem, then I am going to assume it will solve it for me as well.

This is gold. First, it makes people aware of your solution at no cost to you. It reduces or eliminates the friction that prevents people from trying your product, and it motivates them to use it because they know there is value based on their friend's experience. If this works, the power of influence increases. As a result, two friends tell a third friend they love it, and this reduces the friction to conversion again, accelerating adoption. This is the holy grail. No-cost, rapid user adoption and engagement.

The other low-cost way to drive product engagement is to help average users become power users. Investigate what needs to be done to get them to use your product more. Perhaps their needs don't match those of the power users, and therefore, they are already using your product or services to the maximum. For example, they may only use your service eight times a month. Your power users use it twice as much. However, you learn that the users who are using it eight times a month also complement it with another service. Unless you add the other service to your suite, which is something you should consider in the future, you have maxed out this user's usage. Therefore, you should explore acquiring customers that match the power user's profile, because you don't have to change your current offerings.

You can determine the cost to acquire these customers and evaluate it against the costs of building out new services and maintaining them. This analysis will help you determine the most efficient way to build your solutions based on customer and potential-customer interests. This becomes an important analysis because you have limited resources, so you can't do everything at once. You need to establish priorities (to engage power users and get them to spread the word virally) before (time-based decision) you add new features (product road map) to your existing product to help you show strong traction without burning through a lot of cash. It is a fine line, and thoughtful decisions are necessary.

On the other hand, you may have few power users or, worse yet, no power users. This is important to analyze. It is important to recognize that people are not changing their behavior to use your product. You may rationalize it. You may say it needs the new feature or you need better customer reps to explain it or it is the slow time of the year. You may be right, but regardless, you need to really dig in to understand what the root cause is because it may be that your business thesis doesn't match the market. You need to test whether there is truly demand for the product, whether you are targeting the right market, and whether the product delivers value quickly enough (time to value) for the user to use it.

Be very thoughtful about the process, and be as regimented as possible. You want to establish the primary list of items that are causing friction to user adoption and test whether changes will improve usage. Keep this simple. Don't do a complete overhaul of the product or start adding features. Ask the users who are using it the most what they need in order to use it more. Ask users who used it more initially, but discontinued it, why they stopped. Identify a different target market of consumers and ask whether they would use it and why. You are trying to establish the right product for the right target market with the right go-to market strategy. If your first rollout didn't meet expectations, that is ok. However, you don't want to repeat the same mistakes. You want to test new elements to help you refine your approach to eventually get product-market fit.

We covered a lot in this section, so to make it a little easier, I summarized key questions to think about regarding your customer's journey and how they engage with your products or services. After each question, I included a business term that is associated with the question, and I encourage you to explore those topics further if you are unfamiliar with them.

- Who is using it? (user analytics)
- Who is using it a lot? (power user profile)
- Why are they using it a lot? (value proposition)
- What was their path from sign-up to user? (customer journey)
- How much is the value created worth to different users? (value-based pricing)
- Will they use it on an ongoing basis? (recurring usage)
- How long will they pay to use it? (lifetime value)
- Can you get them to use it more? (nurture stream)
- Will they invite and encourage others to use it? (virality)
- Are there others who match the power user profiles who aren't using it but would if they knew about it? (growth marketing)
- How much does it cost to get a user through sales or marketing channels? (customer-acquisition cost)
- Why do people stop using it? (churn)

Understanding your customers, your power users, and their pain points helps you define your "beachhead strategy," which is essential to maximizing gains and minimizing losses. The term "beachhead" is derived from a military strategy that advocates planning and focusing all your resources on winning a small border area, which then becomes a stronghold from which to advance the rest of your troops to take the entire enemy territory. From a new company perspective, it means securing enough initial power users to validate the market demand to build a business in which you will become the market leader. This concept is very important to a new venture because you have limited time and resources to secure the "beach," so you have to prioritize where you focus in order to be highly effective and reach your goals.

# COMMUNICATE WITH PURPOSE

When you start telling customers, future employees, and the press about your business, you need to quickly explain the value it delivers *and* the purpose behind it. Done well, this allows you to immediately grab people's interest. We call this your **Purpose Promise**. Think of it as your "elevator pitch" infused with a perfect dose of purpose.

Your Purpose Promise helps connect your value proposition with the heart and soul of the company—its purpose. It explains how your company delivers more than just a valuable product or service, but also how you are making a meaningful impact on the world. Below is an example of a Purpose Promise for PurposeCo, the hypothetical company we are following, and their product, the PurposeCo App.

> *PurposeCo reduces stress in an increasingly stressful world. We help busy professionals lower their anxiety to live better lives. Our PurposeCo App is like a personal coach that is with you 24/7. Unlike other fitness wearables that focus on counting steps, PurposeCo helps deploy stress-reducing techniques to calm you and avoid stress-induced bad habits. When you need a little additional help, PurposeCo connects you to a certified healthcare professional who will guide you through a proven stress-reducing process to get you back on track. PurposeCo helps you reduce stress, improve your health, and live your best life.*

Pillars. Then, you need to align their performance with the overall performance of the organization. This ensures the company, teams, and individuals are always purposefully aligned toward achieving the top strategic goals and meeting the key performance indicator metrics (KPIs). Purpose helps drive outstanding performance, and it is optimized when everyone knows what is expected, when it is expected, and how they are evaluated.

Setting top strategic goals should be simple. Don't over-complicate it. What are the top five to ten objectives you want to accomplish over time? Strategic goals may be a mix of financial or nonfinancial. However, they must be measurable and tie to how they will achieve your vision.

While strategic goals are important, KPI dashboards—or "objectives and key results" (OKR) dashboards—significantly improve your ability to measure and manage the overall performance of the business on an ongoing basis. By creating a simple dashboard of the most important aspects of the business, one that is updated on a regular basis, you will be able to foster fast-paced, fact-based decision-making while allowing for visibility and insights into the business, which allows the entire team to make more informed, strategic decisions. This will assure the performance of your entire team drives the growth of your Purpose First Business.

Let's apply this goal setting and performance measurement process to PurposeCo.

PurposeCo's *long-term goal* is to be the number-one health technology company in reducing work-related stress in corporate America within ten years of formal launch. They know selling to companies can take a long time and be complicated. However, they also know selling to companies can ensure their employees will get the product at a very low cost or even for free. This will accelerate product adoption.

They set a *mid-term goal* to have 24 self-insured companies using the PurposeCo App with a 55% employee adoption rate within 24 months of formal launch. These goals help set the company's sights for the future. And of course, they can be revisited and adjusted up or down as they are in market. Their *near-term goals* are to recruit the team necessary to launch the beta over the course of the next three months, to successfully release the full version of the PuproseCo App by the end of year, and to be able to quantify the work-related stress reduction for all of their clients to validate the efficacy of the product.

At first, PurposeCo is focused on getting the beta ready and busting their butts to convince their first few customers to try their pilot. However, once things start moving, they will be sure to set up their KPIs. They will focus on how many self-insured companies sign up for the service, how many of their employees are successfully using the product, how quickly those employees demonstrate a measurable improvement in stress reduction, and how those improvements translate into cost reductions for the company. These four KPIs will allow the entire organization to quantify how they perform in honoring the company's Purpose Vision, Purpose Promise, and Purpose Pillars.

Then the next three KPIs will help determine how effectively they are performing to build a scalable business from an economic perspective. These subsequent KPIs will focus on how much it costs to acquire a new client, how long it takes for the new client to offset the costs to acquire them, and how efficiently the team scales to support profitable growth.

Once PurposeCo has established the organization goals and KPIs, the organization will assign roles and responsibilities to achieve the objectives to the appropriate departments, teams, and individuals. Everyone should clearly understand what is expected of them so that they can perform their jobs successfully, and how their work contributes to PurposeCo's success. Even if you're already an experienced entrepreneur, it's important to revisit this information from time to time to tune up your business.

As a Purpose First Entrepreneur, you must ensure that *purpose* intersects with *performance* and vice versa. They must be married to yield the results needed to successful.

# CHAPTER 6

# FUNDING YOUR PURPOSE FIRST BUSINESS

Your goal is to build a successful Purpose First Business, not to raise capital. Some entrepreneurs get that confused because fundraising can be glamorized (think *Shark Tank*). However, when you are starting off, it may be difficult because you don't have much revenue to cover your expenses. This prevents a lot of people from starting a business. But don't let it stop you; there are different paths you can take to solve this problem. Let's pause, get back to the basics, and talk through the ins and outs of several different funding options for starting your Purpose First Business.

**❶ ATTENTION, PLEASE:** The National Venture Capital Association (NVCA) is a great resource for learning more about start-up financing. They are the authority for standardization of the legal documents for the venture capital industry. Another resource that will help you get oriented around this topic is Brad Feld and Jason Mendelson's book, *Venture Deals: Be Smarter Than Your Lawyer and Venture Capitalist.*

# BOOTSTRAP IT

I recommend you try to validate your model without spending money. As I discussed in the previous chapter, confirm there is user demand for your product or service. Once done, you have some options to start market testing. The more you can self-fund at this point, the better. But what if you don't have any money? Well ... that makes it harder.

First, don't quit your day job! Keep it. Save money and focus on your business whenever you can. Get up early. Work late. Work on the weekends. Just make sure you are setting goals and making progress. Next, keep your costs down as much as possible. Don't spend unless you absolutely have to. For example, use free software trials to test your business. In other words, hold off until you're ready to test your idea, then sign up for the free software option many companies offer. Don't convert to the paid subscription until you validate some of the key elements of your business.

This frugal mindset will help you run a capital-efficient business from day one. Keep in mind, it doesn't have to be perfect when you are testing an idea; it just has to be good enough to show that there is interest. Most people who try your product or service early are not looking for something perfect. They know they are an early customer and are typically trusting you more than the services, so they are forgiving. By keeping your costs down, you can really stretch your dollars a lot further than you'd think.

The same goes for people. In the very beginning, don't start paying people until you have to. I don't mean don't pay people for what they are doing for you. However, in the beginning, save your cash if you can. If you don't know something, search and learn. There are a variety of entrepreneur-focused publications that post free articles and information on their websites, such as *Entrepreneur, Inc.*, and *foundr,* or check out venture capital firms' sites like First Round Capital and a16z.[7] They all have practical lessons that can be quickly applied to your business.

Furthermore, those learnings will also give you a baseline for the type of skills you need when you are ready to start hiring. Once you get an understanding of what you need, you can start talking to folks who are qualified to do what you need them to do. Those conversations will help validate your business thesis while filling the talent queue to open when you have the cash to start hiring full time.

If you absolutely need to hire someone, try to have them start off on a freelance basis. It will help you control your costs. If your business grows, then you can bring them on full time. This process will help to ensure they are aligned with you and the Purpose First Business you are building. And, just as important, you'll know they are capable of contributing immediately.

Creating an advisory board of experts who are aligned with your Purpose Vision is also a great way to get powerful insights without spending money. Your passion and purpose will help attract the right folks who have a proven track record of success in your industry. Their expertise will be extremely valuable growing your business.

Advisors will also be able to use their reputations and networks to give you more credibility with key stakeholders; as a result, they will help you recruit talent, attract customers and partners, and even fundraise, if needed. The commitments you are asking of them will drive how formal this group should be. The more requests you make, the more likely it is you will have to think of a form of compensation that is appropriate. Often you don't have to pay them at the beginning. If they ask to be paid in the form of cash or equity, you should really make that determination based on how much value they bring. You will want to ensure they are truly valuable and will deliver before you compensate them.

I can't emphasize enough that bootstrapping can be powerful. It allows you to retain all the equity and control of your business. The more you grow without raising capital, the more options you have. In contrast, raising capital may help fuel growth, which also has its advantages and disadvantages. You will have to decide based on your circumstances.

# BEYOND BOOTSTRAPPING

Assuming you've done everything I recommended and you still need capital, or you want to accelerate growth because your business is rocking it … where do you start? Well, look in the mirror. Do you have money? If the answer is yes, then invest in the business. However, don't be hell-bent on risking all your money; you want to balance it out. Here's why. If you risk all your dough and your business fails, you may be in a situation that is extremely difficult to recover from.

I realize some of you have an all-in mentality and you are ready to bet all. I encourage you to really think about your risk-reward ratio and be clear about the downside scenario, especially if you are using personal credit to finance it. So be willing to put money in, but don't be afraid to invite others to help finance your business. It mitigates the risk for you, and if it is successful, everyone will make money. We will explore this in more detail, but before we do, let's explore a few other options.

Investigate alternative programs from which you may positioned to secure seed capital. Some may even be looking for purpose driven companies just like yours. Here are some options to consider:

1. Participate in a pitch competition sponsored by a university, company, or venture firm.

2. Apply for the next class to join a start-up accelerator like Yellow, 500 Start-ups, or Ycombinator.[8]

3. Investigate opportunities to secure capital through organizations targeting specific types of founders such as Future Founders, TECHRISE, GET Cities, or Bunker Labs, which offer resources based on specific criteria.[9] If you aren't aware of local or national programs like these, check sites like American Inno, Startup Grind, or TechCrunch.[10] They often feature accelerators, pitch contests, and other programs you may qualify for.

However, don't get too caught up in applying for accelerators and start-up contests because you may end up investing time pitching your business rather than building your business. I realize that it can be a catch-22. However, make sure whatever you engage in will add value to your business. The top programs will provide a wealth of information that will help you build your business. The low-tier programs are often a waste of time.

The U.S. Small Business Administration (SBA) is another option to explore.[11] They have some interesting resources for starting your business. The federal government also offers grants for specific initiatives, such as the $60 million of funding through the US Department of Energy and US Office of Energy Efficiency and Renewable Energy, which is focused on priorities in batteries and electrification, advanced engine and fuel technologies, and new mobility technologies.[12]

Other good resources to explore when searching for financing are local entrepreneurs and innovation centers that are operated by a mix of academic, public, and private collaborations. For example, Chicago has P33, Discovery Partner Institute, Northwestern's The Garage, University of Chicago Polsky Center, 1871, Matter, mHUB, Portal Innovations, The Hatchery—and that is just to name a few.[13] If you're not near a metropolitan area that has these types of resources, go online. Many of these organizations have great digital programs too.

## Tax Incentives for New Businesses

Depending on the business entity—C corporation (C corp), S corporation (S corp), limited liability corporation (LLC)—and type of investment that is made, there are often federal tax incentives for new businesses to consider, such as IRS Code Section 1202: Qualified Small Business Stock Exemption, and state tax incentives, such as the Illinois Angel Investment Tax Credit Program. These programs are designed to help entrepreneurs attract investors in the early stages of their companies, when it's often hardest to bring investors on board, by providing tax incentives to encourage investments in start-ups. The government creates these types of tax incentives because start-ups are one of the top sources for job growth and help drive the national, state, and local economies. Understanding what you are eligible for and ensuring you are maximizing the advantages you qualify for is a great way to create incentives for people to invest.

# VISIT A LOCAL BANK

We can keep this one short and sweet.

It is unlikely this is the best option because they typically require personal assets to collateralize your business loan. However, you should evaluate your local bank financing options because you may qualify for special programs they have. It is also possible your banker may know of other credible local organization who might invest in small businesses like yours.

# UNDERSTAND THE ROUNDS

If you start looking for venture capital, you need to understand the fundamentals. The first stage of venture financing is often

fortunate to have a few friends or connections that have some money to invest, they may be a good source of cash to help start your business. These individuals know you better than anyone else. They trust you and know what you are capable of. They're likely to be very supportive of your purpose and of your taking this big step.

# ENGAGE ANGEL INVESTORS

Many entrepreneurs don't know the difference between angel investors and venture capital firms. Simply put, angel investors write checks from their personal banking accounts. Venture capital firms, which we'll discuss in the next section, write checks from the firm's "banking account" on behalf of their investors.

Angel investors vary in sophistication and value. I recommend working with angels who understand the venture industry. It helps ensure you're aligned with industry standards, which is important for future financing. The best angels offer more than money. They contribute expertise, connections, and resources that fuel growth. Some angels write smaller checks, so you have to make sure they create enough value to be worth your time. I realize you may say, "WTF, Pete, I need the money." Well, you don't need the money from someone who may prevent you from being successful because they waste your time, create no value, or have not bought into your Purpose Vision.

"Super Angels" are individuals who are more sophisticated investors with deeper pockets and greater expertise. They can be extremely valuable, but they can suck too. They may seem great, but you still need to reference-check them—this is true for all investors, including VCs. You want to talk to the founders they previously backed. You may hear great things, but you may learn that they were controlling and their financing terms were onerous. Just because they are giving you money doesn't mean they will act like an angel. It is your job to do your homework on them before you take their money.

Angel groups are similar to angel investors. Unlike solo angel investors, groups aggregate investors' money to invest in your company. They typically invest more capital in a deal than a single angel. The best groups have a strong reputation for helping founders grow their businesses into industry leaders. They leverage their collective human capital to maximize the financial capital. This formula delivers the fuel the founders need to be successful. The best angel groups in the country create enormous value for early-stage companies, often equal to national top-tier VC firms. To find an angel group in your area, I recommend visiting the Angel Capital Association membership directory.[15]

Regardless of whether it is an angel, angel group, or venture capital firm, you need to understand what type of businesses they invest in. Many have an investment thesis about a specific sector or geographic region or a particular stage of investment—like the seed stage. You want to maximize your time by understanding what they are looking for. The closer you match their profile, the more likely you are to be considered. I will provide some additional details on the process later, but now I want to help explain the stage of investment.

Do your homework regardless of where you get your investments. You want to make sure there are clear processes in place for funding and post-investment support to help you scale your business. As you do your due diligence, talk to founders who were successful and those who failed. Find out how they felt they were treated. Make sure that the angels you're choosing to work with seem inclined to support both your business and the purpose that underpins it. Angel groups can be a great option if you pick the right one.

# EXPLORE VENTURE CAPITAL

Often entrepreneurs get caught up in seeking venture capital funding. It becomes their goal. They think it validates their business. Don't think this way! Growth validates your business. Revenue validates your business. And most importantly, profit validates your business. Your focus is growing your business. If your business consistently grows, capital will likely find you.

You may create more wealth for yourself by building a small business that consistently generates positive cash flow than by trying to build a much bigger business through venture financing. Once you take venture capital, the pressure to grow increases, and your ownership decreases. However, your business may be one that can be the next ShipBob, G2, or Airbnb, and you need capital to grow to truly capture the opportunity. Thus, venture capital may help you realize your full potential and become an industry leader in a cost-effective way, which will create wealth, and every now and then, a new billionaire.

The faster you grow, and the greater the potential for you to efficiently grow much bigger, the greater the value of your company. That statement is ridiculously simple for something that can be very complicated. But growth is paramount. And most VC firms are betting that your company will become an industry leader. To get to a valuation, they are using other companies' values as market comparables (similar to when you shop for a house) as a starting point. Then, they validate that logic by modeling the future growth of your company based on different growth scenarios, typically creating models ranging from aggressive to conservative. As a result, different firms will have different perspectives on your value, which is why some firms pass on investing altogether and other firms provide term sheets that value your business much differently.

The valuation of your company is important to you as a founder. In a simple example, let's say you own 100% of the shares of your company, and after negotiations with an investor, it is agreed upon that your company is valued at $20M. (Awesome! You went from having zero value when you started—not bad.) That agreed-upon valuation establishes the calculations for ownership post-investment. If the VC invests $5M, now your company will be worth $25M ($20M + $5M). After the investment, the VC now owns 20% ($5M/$25M) of your company, and you own 80% ($20M/$25M) of your company. To be clear, the value of your ownership is now $20M, so although you own less of the company percentage-wise, the value in absolute dollars of what you own has increased significantly.

Although valuation is important, the terms of your financing and the decision-making in running your business will be shared with the investors. Investors can put in a variety of terms that impact how much money you will make if you sell your business and, just as importantly, how you can run your business, finance your business, and grow your business, and you need to understand these terms. Be sure to have a good lawyer with experience in venture financing. If you need help finding one, you may want to reach out to your local NVCA's regional group.[16]

You may have the best lawyer and an awesome business, but if you have the wrong VC firm, you could have a big problem. Many people liken it to marriage. However, it is a lot easier to get divorced from your life partner than get divorced from your investor in business. Furthermore, you are not really marrying the firm that is investing in you. You are marrying the partner of the firm who is leading the financing and who is joining your board. Therefore, you need to do your due diligence on both the firm and the partner.

Venture firms certainly evaluate you. A study published in the March/April 2021 issue of the *Harvard Business Review* explains it really well:

> Even for entrepreneurs who do gain access to a VC, the odds of securing funding are exceedingly low. Our survey found that for each deal a VC firm eventually closes, the firm considers, on average, 101 opportunities. Twenty-eight of those opportunities will lead to a meeting with management; 10 will be reviewed at a partner meeting; 4.8 will proceed to due diligence; 1.7 will move on to the negotiations of a term sheet with the start-up, and only one will actually be funded.

A typical deal takes 83 days to close, and firms reported spending an average of 118 hours of due diligence during that period, making calls to an average of 10 references.[17]

There are a lot of great angels, early-stage investors, and VCs out there. They come in different shapes and sizes. However, if you find the right one(s), they will significantly help turn your Purpose First Business into an incredible success.

# CHAPTER 7

# HOW TO PERFORM AT AN ELITE LEVEL

Venture capitalists uniformly agree *founders*—and ultimately their *performance*—are the most important factor in a start-up's success. So why don't more entrepreneurs focus on performing at an elite level? You should! Let's dig into *how to perform at an elite level.*

After meeting with thousands of founders and investing in hundreds of them, I've seen a broad range of successes and failures. I wondered why. So I started to dig into the data and began to ask: how do entrepreneurs optimize their performance to be successful? How do they improve their results over time? Is there a formula for success? If so, what variables truly matter to drive the best results?

As a Purpose First Entrepreneur, you will set personal and professional goals you want to achieve. You should start to think of it kind of like an equation. Your performance, or the actions you take to achieve a goal, will yield a result. Based on your performance, your results will fall within a spectrum of possibilities ranging from 100% success to 100% failure. While sometimes you will absolutely succeed or fail, most often you will fall somewhere within that range.

For example, let's say your goal is to get ten new customers but you got seven. You didn't hit your goal, but you didn't outright fail. It is relative to your circumstances and depends on the overall progress you are making toward your desired outcome. The **Results Formula** diagram helps illustrate how your performance drives results that fall along a spectrum of success and failure.

## Results Formula

$$\frac{\textbf{Goals}}{\textbf{Performance}} = \textbf{RESULTS} \begin{cases} \text{Success} \\ \updownarrow \\ \text{Failure} \end{cases}$$

As an entrepreneur, you don't want perfection to be the enemy of progress. You'll have to determine whether your performance against your short-term goal moved you closer to your long-term goal. You might not hit 100% of your goal (e.g., seven new customers out of ten), but seven new customers certainly allowed you to meaningfully advance your business. At the same time, failing to hit your goal may have also surfaced a critical performance issue that you need to correct in order to be successful in the longer term.

The further you are from your desired outcome, the more performance adjustments you'll need to make. For example, perhaps you wanted to hire four software engineers to accelerate the development of your product. After six months, you only have one. You'll need to really dig in to determine why your performance is off on attracting the necessary talent, or maybe even reconsider your strategy, such as changing your approach and outsourcing an engineering team versus hiring one.

If you don't adjust your performance and solve for this recruiting failure, it will negatively impact your business—maybe some of your current customers will walk away because your initial product is not meeting their needs. The **Optimize Your Performance** diagram helps visualize the concept of appropriately adjusting your performance based on your results.

## Optimize Your Performance

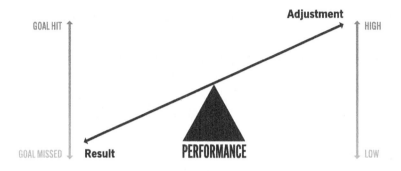

Optimizing your performance is often more complicated than just doing one or two things differently. For example, your circumstances may have the biggest impact on your performance. To help illustrate this point, let's say you're a competitive 100m sprinter. What if you know the best training for competitive 100m sprinters is across the country with the top trainers in the world? Given elite athletes in highly competitive races win by just a hair, everything matters. Despite this, you decide to train locally with the best trainers in your region. Will your performance be impacted by the decision about where you train? If you don't achieve the results you want, you have to take that into consideration after the race, when you evaluate performance. You have to evaluate not just your ability, but the decisions you made about training, and whether they proved favorable or unfavorable in you performing at your best.

# PURPOSE FIRST PERFORMANCE EQUATION

Elevating your performance to an elite level depends on multiple factors. But what are they? If you understood them, you could improve your probability of success. Similar to an elite sprinter, where every second counts, the same could be true for entrepreneurs, where many decisions may make or break you.

I mapped out what worked and didn't work in the start-ups that I was a part of and the businesses I ran. I compared that against the hundreds of founders my early-stage venture group invested in. I overlaid those learnings against the countless successful and unsuccessful start-ups that I've written about in *Forbes* and engaged with over the past few decades in the entrepreneurial ecosystem.

I put those learnings side-by-side with my knowledge of historical figures who have achieved incredible results. I studied the top civic leaders of our time (like Nelson Mandela and Malala Yousafzai), world-changing mathematicians (like Albert Einstein and Katherine Johnson), sports legends (like Michael Jordan and Simone Biles), as well as business luminaries (like Steve Jobs and Arianna Huffington).

I analyzed performance training for elite athletes, special-ops forces, and corporate executives. I collected evidence, both qualitative and quantitative, to truly understand in a pragmatic and philosophical way.

So, after my tireless pursuit to uncover the secret ingredient of greatness, I am proud to reveal the most common variable across all elite performers is… PURPOSE. When people have a clear purpose that relentlessly drives them, it undoubtedly enhances their performance, regardless of their abilities and circumstances.

Purpose improves everyone's performance. It drives the ordinary to be extraordinary, and the elite to become legendary. In mathematical terms, purpose has an exponential impact on performance. The rate of your enhanced performance correlates to the intrinsic value of your purpose itself. The more powerful your purpose, the more it motivates you to keep making the necessary decisions to achieve your goals, regardless of the setbacks, failures, and challenges. And, just as importantly, it propels you to challenge yourself to do even more after experiencing success.

Based on my findings, I developed the Purpose First Performance Equation. The concepts behind the equation were known, taught, and applied long before me. I simply organized them so that I could more effectively share them with others. They are less about guaranteeing success and more about creating a framework for personal performance improvement.

## Purpose First Performance Equation

$$\text{PERFORMANCE} = \text{DECISION}^{\text{Purpose}} \; (\text{ACTION} \times \text{ABILITY} \times \text{CIRCUMSTANCE})$$

The **Purpose First Performance Equation** explains how the strength of your **purpose** exponentially influences your **decision** to **act**, based on your **ability** to perform, and the **circumstances** in which you are performing to achieve your goals. Although purpose may significantly elevate your performance to an elite level, your decisions ultimately drive it. This creates the fundamental concepts in the Purpose First Performance Equation.

As a Purpose First Entrepreneur, how do you use the performance equation? Well, let's apply it to PurposeCo. Below is PurposeCo's Purpose Promise (developed in Chapter 5).

*PurposeCo reduces stress in an increasingly stressful world. We help busy professionals lower their anxiety to live better lives. Our PurposeCo App is like a personal coach who is with you 24/7. Unlike other fitness wearables that focus on counting steps, PurposeCo helps deploy stress-reducing techniques to calm you and avoid stress-induced bad habits. When you need a little additional help, PurposeCo connects you to a certified healthcare professional who will guide you through a proven stress-reducing process to get you back on track. PurposeCo helps you reduce stress, improve your health, and live your best life.*

The founder's primary goal is to successfully build PurposeCo into a sustainable and profitable business. Let's use the Purpose First Performance Equation to help her assess her situation at the starting point.

We know her Purpose Vision and Purpose Pillars are fully aligned with PurposeCo's Purpose Promise to empower people to reduce stress, improve health, and live their best lives. She lives and breathes it. Her purpose is strong.

Her purpose had a major influence on her decision to act. She founded PurposeCo. Her purpose helped her overcome a big fear of quitting her job, the simmering anxiety of the unknown, and the recurring doubts about her ability to run a business. Nevertheless, her drive to do something that was truly purposeful helped her overcome those risks, and she made the decision to do it. After completing all the work necessary to get ready to launch her business, she filed the paperwork for PurposeCo to become a legal entity.

Again, her decision to act—file the paperwork—meant she was officially starting PurposeCo. It was very conscious and deeply purposeful. It was more than filing paperwork. It represented a clear action to make her vision a reality. This action prompted other important decisions. She started telling her friends and other people about PurposeCo, which made her feel more accountable to herself and others to perform at her best to make it a reality.

That's where her next set of important Purpose First Performance Equation decisions came in. She evaluated her abilities in running the company. In relation to her goal of becoming a successful founder, she listed the abilities she needed to be successful—where she had the most experience, skills, and competencies. Then she reflected on her mental, physical, and emotional strengths and weaknesses to be an effective leader.

She decided that she would focus on leaning into what she does well, leading people. She became the CEO. This decision created the best circumstances for her to succeed. She would recruit a diversely talented team to complement each other. They would each have a role that made the team stronger because they were able to focus on their strengths, filling each other's gaps, and ultimately creating a high-performance team.

See, she had already started to control the circumstances she could control. She decided on a strength-driven talent recruitment philosophy in order to build the team. (Many times we can't control the team we are a part of, but as a Purpose First Entrepreneur, we can.) The team she recruits will directly influence her performance, as well as their own and the organization's.

Upon reflection, she realized she had an "everyone works from the office mindset" from her previous job. Catching this bias was critical. As a result, she decided, with the new model, her team can work virtually. This decision allows her to improve her circumstances, enabling her to cost-effectively recruit talent from across the globe. Furthermore, this decision is directly aligned with her, and the company's, Purpose Pillars. It creates the right circumstances for her team to spend less time commuting and more time acting on things that matter to them. The value of the approach became even more apparent as a result of the pandemic, which forced employees to work from home. The circumstances weren't controllable—like many in life—however, she learned that the response to the new normal was within her control.

Thanks to the PurposeCo founder example, you have an understanding of how the Purpose First Performance Equation works. Let's dig in further to see the applications in your own life.

As you embark on your journey to create your Purpose First Business and improve the quality of both your personal and professional lives, you can use the Purpose First Performance Equation to maximize your performance and subsequent results by aligning your goals with what is important to you, making purposeful decisions, and making adjustments to further optimize your performance.

Let me provide an example of the Purpose First Performance Equation in life, and how the right decision about changing my circumstance played out for me.

After my mom died when I was 10, I started acting out at school. I can remember going to Woodrow Wilson School. I was very small for my age. At the time, this school was in a rough neighborhood. The rules on the playground were more likely settled by fighting than talking it out. I often felt that I needed to defend my territory, and being small, I had a lot of defending to do.

Well, one day I was getting harassed by a couple of kids in class. I completely lost it when one of the kids who was screwing with me hit me. I'd had enough and pushed him as hard as I could. He stumbled back, and the desk behind him tipped over. As it did, he fell backward. His legs flipped up, and the back of his head hit the floor with incredible velocity. As he hit the floor, the teacher walked in. The teacher saw it all. That was bad news for me.

After meeting with the principal, my dad knew he had to do something. Although he didn't think about it in Purpose First Performance Equation terms, he used it. He knew he needed to act to achieve his goal—to put me in the best position to succeed before the wheels started coming off and I ended up in a juvenile detention center.

He thought putting me in the right environment—or creating better circumstances for me—would help me develop. He thought the values of a Catholic school would provide what I needed and that the people who were running it would put me in the most nurturing environment. This would improve my dad's ability to help me grow as a person, core to his purpose. However, my dad was a blue-collar refinery worker, so paying the tuition made things really, really hard financially. Like so many parents, he was willing to sacrifice anything to help me live a better life.

When my dad told me his Catholic school decision, I lost it. I didn't think about the great teachers, the strong curriculum, and the nurturing culture. I thought about how much my friends in public school hated the Catholic-school kids. I thought about how we used to stand by the alley that separated our public-school yard from the Catholic-school yard and yell back and forth. I was going to be a Catholic-school kid, the worst of the worst in my mind. I actually thought about running away so I didn't have to face the humiliation of walking by my public-school friends on my way into the Catholic school. At the time, I couldn't conceive of anything worse.

But hats off to my dad, who withstood all the animosity that I directed toward him, which was pretty fierce (think of the flamethrower of pre-adolescent fury). I pretty much told him daily that I hated him. Thinking back upon it, as a dad myself now, I realize it must have been horrible. His wife had recently died, and his youngest son hated him for making a really tough decision, and all he was trying to do was help.

I was unwilling to see my new circumstance as an opportunity to grow and get stronger. Instead, I saw it as a threat. I was unwilling to change my mindset and embrace my new circumstances because I was more comfortable where I was—as bad as it was— than I was willing to be uncomfortable in a new environment.

Surprisingly, as humans, we do this every day.

We stay comfortable in inaction because deciding to act is too scary. But when we tap into our purpose and take control of our decisions and focus on the variables that improve our performance, great things can and will happen.

As humans, we have unique power to decide. The tough question often is, are we willing to make that decision—the decision to improve our abilities or circumstances?

My dad was willing to make that critical decision. It was a hard choice for him, as I described. But a decision was made, and thanks to my father, it changed my life. It changed my circumstances and sent me on a different trajectory. Although my path through middle school was far from a fairytale from that point forward, it did offer me a new path. It wasn't until decades later, after studying performance, that I realized the impact my dad's decision had on my life and the opportunities it provided me.

As humans, we must be aware of the opportunities to adjust our Purpose First Performance Equation, and to improve the results we earn. However, we must have the courage to be extraordinary—

not ordinary—to make decisions that many people would never make. Success is not easy. It is about being accountable to yourself and showing up every day. Although your best does not always equal success, it will put you in the best position to lead a life that is well-lived every day.

## MAXIMIZE YOUR PERFORMANCE

The Purpose First Performance Equation is being constantly applied to your life. It is a theory you can apply to all aspects. It is much more circular than it is linear, as shown in the **Purposeful Improvement Loop** diagram. Unlike a mathematical equation that is solved only once, the Purpose First Performance Equation is constantly evolving. You can use the Purpose First Performance Equation as a personal methodology to allow you to perform at your best to achieve your goals.

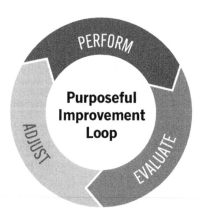

By evaluating and managing the key performance variables, you will maximize your performance to help you reach a single goal, multiple goals, or a sustainable and satisfying career and life. The steps are simple:

- Set a goal.
- Perform to achieve the goal.
- If the result achieves your goal, then celebrate your success!
- If the result doesn't achieve the goal, then make necessary adjustments to one or more of the Purpose First Performance Equation variables to improve your performance to reach your goal.

In order to improve, you must regularly evaluate how you perform. You must take into account how decisions drive the appropriate actions, with or without the necessary abilities, given the circumstances at the time of the decision. Therefore, to optimize your performance, you have to concentrate on enhancing these variables to determine the impact on the result.

## PURPOSE FIRST PERFORMANCE EQUATION VARIABLES

# PURPOSE

I've talked a lot about purpose and how it turns the ordinary into the extraordinary. I've explained how to establish your Purpose Vision and Purpose Pillars. Now I will explain how to use it in relation to the Purpose First Performance Equation to improve your performance to achieve your goals.

Purpose has an exponential impact on our decisions. When we can see it, sense it, and feel it, it will positively power decisions. When our purpose is strong, clear, and present, we will have clarity on the decisions we must make to drive the necessary actions we must take to perform at our best.

The process of finding our purpose is often easier than acting with purpose. Our purpose can wane when we get rejected, encounter obstacles, or flat out fail. Our purpose can get pushed to the background as our lives get busy and obligations mount. In order to tap into the power of purpose, we must be in tune with it. Our attention needs to be calibrated to harnessing the power of our purpose in every decision we make that advances us toward our goal.

To successfully make decisions that matter, our purpose needs to be fully centered in our minds. We have to train our minds to keep our purpose present. Like an athlete whose elite performance in a game comes from the training and practices before the game, we need to establish daily routines to build mental muscle to keep our purpose in our minds. We want it to be as natural as LeBron James shooting a basketball. Our practice will help us keep our purpose in the forefront of our minds when we need it to perform at our best.

Our performance is optimized when we are fully aware of our purpose in the decisions we make that matter. I'm not talking about all decisions—like choosing between a blue shirt or red shirt. I am talking about the ones that *matter*. The ones that truly drive our performance.

I encourage you to turn this abstract idea of purpose and frame it so you can see it. Envision the emotions you will feel upon achieving your goal. It helps you hardwire your purpose into your brain's neural pathways. Define what it is and understand the intimate details of how you want to feel and expect others to feel when it becomes a reality. Imagine it. Use that image as your motivation to overcome the obstacles and stay relentlessly intentional to reach your goal. The more you can see it and feel it, the more likely it is to become a reality. For this to truly work, your goals have to be outrageously meaningful to you. They must intrinsically motivate you to overcome challenges that inevitably arise.

How intentional you are every day in being purpose driven will have the biggest impact on your long-term performance. Create a simple routine to remind yourself what you are trying to achieve and why. This will help you connect to your purpose and keep it present in your decision-making throughout the day. The more purposeful your decisions, the more likely you are to achieve your desired results.

So now let's put this into practice.

Sam is a Purpose First Entrepreneur. He has been building his personal training business for the past 11 months. He is making just enough money to cover his bills. The strain of trying to attract new clients while learning new business skills is really impacting him. His days start at 4:30 a.m. to get ready for his first client. The grind is really starting to take a toll.

He is thinking about quitting and going back to his old job. He reflects on how easy it was just to show up and do the same thing every day. He reminisces about getting to work at 9:00 a.m. and taking a long lunch.

Then one day is especially bad. His first client texted him 10 minutes after his 5:30 a.m. appointment was supposed to start. It read: "Sorry, I can't make it. Please don't charge me." Later, the gym owner told Sam that he has to increase his monthly gym fee. Finally, as the day was ending, he accidentally deleted the monthly newsletter he had been working on for the past two hours. He hangs his head and thinks, *I'm not sure I can do this…*

He starts contemplating a big decision—a life-changing decision—one that really matters. He is thinking about shutting down his business. To provide some additional context, Sam previously worked as a field rep for a utility business. Prior to that, he graduated with a B.S. in Kinesiology from a Big Ten University and was the strength coach for one of the state's top football teams. He is passionate about fitness and health. Not only did he love it, but the people he trained also loved him and the results he was able to help them achieve.

There are aspects of Sam's Purpose First Performance Equation that he needs to reevaluate, but the biggest variable that is impacting his decision today is connecting to his purpose. He decided to pursue his own personal training business because it made a difference in his life and the lives of others. It was completely aligned with his Purpose Pillars. Furthermore, he was good at it and had a good reputation in the industry.

Sam has to reconnect with his purpose.

He needs to reflect. How meaningful is being a personal trainer to him? Is building his training business aligned with his Purpose Vision and Purpose Pillars? Is it a must-have or nice-to-have for him? How intentional is he every day in making it happen? Is he motivated enough to overcome challenges?

If Sam answers yes to these questions, he knows that his purpose is still driving him, and he should continue. He should dig in. However, he still has work to do. He needs to evaluate all the other Purpose First Performance Equation variables to decide what else he needs to focus on.

Does he need to improve his ability to run a training business? We know he doesn't need to improve his training skills or knowledge. Perhaps he needs help with digital marketing to cost-effectively attract new clients? Or maybe he needs to change his circumstances. Perhaps he moves his gym near the high school where he was a well-respected trainer so it is easier for the people he knows to use him. Or maybe he needs to move out of the suburbs to the city, where the population of potential clients is denser?

These are all decisions that impact his performance. They will directly impact his ability to achieve his goal of building a successful personal training business. However, if his purpose is not aligned with his goal, he should certainly reevaluate his decision to run a personal training business, because it is very unlikely he will have the fortitude to overcome all the changes he will encounter to do it.

# DECISIONS

If purpose is the "heart," then decisions are the "brains" of the Purpose First Performance Equation. Purpose will motivate us to make tough decisions, powerful decisions, and intentional decisions. Our brains may tell us, *No, that's too hard, too challenging, or too scary*. But our purpose will override those fears and elevate our decision-making to a higher level.

When we are making purposeful decisions, we have clarity. We decide to act, not to act, or to wait to act. The more intentional we are about those decisions, the more aware we are of the results of our decisions. The more we are aware of the results, the more opportunity we have to continuously improve.

Some decisions we spend a lot of time on. For example, some people may spend a lot of time contemplating their decision to start a company. However, many of our decisions are made in the blink of an eye, like the decision to get a dog. Both decisions will have a material impact on our lives. Our decisions are personal, loaded with biases and imperfections. But the more aware we are of making decisions, the more likely our decision-making will improve.

Some people will argue many things are out of our control. I would agree. We don't have control over many circumstances—for example, the global pandemic. However, we do have control over the decisions we make once our circumstances change. We may decide to take advantage of some freed-up time to create a plan to start a business.

You cannot control the uncontrollable, but you can control your decisions. When I got hit in the head with a club, my circumstances completely changed. At the time, I would have argued that my life was permanently altered for the worse. I lost my short-term memory, couldn't talk in full sentences, and could barely walk a straight line. In retrospect, my decision not to give up made me who I am today. It was also a catalyst for deciding to become an entrepreneur.

However, those choices became decisions that I made after my circumstances changed. I controlled those decisions. I could have said, "Screw it! My life is not under my control. Why bother?" But I reset. My decisions were based on my new normal. And after time, my decisions led to new and more favorable circumstances.

*If we don't like the results, we have the power to change them through our decisions.*

If purpose is the "heart" and decisions are the "brains," think of abilities as the rest of your "body." They are what you are born with. It is up to you to improve them. We all have a different baseline of abilities. Some people are naturally smarter, stronger, or more emotionally aware, just like some people are shorter or taller. You can't decide to grow taller. However, you can decide to use your height (short or tall) as an advantage. For example, you can choose to pursue a sport where being short is an advantage.

Either scenario requires a decision. Based on your decision, you will have to improve your skills to succeed. You will have to practice to get better. This decision to get better will improve your physical abilities, your expertise, and your competency. These are all decisions that improve your ability and improve the performance that helps you succeed.

So decisions drive the Purpose First Performance Equation. They drive everything we do—whether they are made consciously or unconsciously. Therefore, one of the easiest things to do to improve decision-making is to create awareness around it. Become mindful. This fosters awareness of intent. Once we know we are making a decision, we are in a better place to make more purposeful decisions. Ones that are intentional and aligned with our purpose and desired outcomes. Our purposeful decisions control the goals we set, and ultimately, how we perform to achieve them.

As you might imagine, the more aware you are of your decisions, the more effective you are.

One way to align your thought process is with a simple **Purpose First Decision Tree**. Ask yourself, *What is my desired outcome? Is my intention appropriate? Will my decision be purposeful?* After going through your decision tree, pull the trigger and act. This process sparks your performance toward reaching your desired outcome. We'll talk more about decision-making in Chapter 9.

## Purpose First Decision Tree
Making Good Decisions

→ What is my desired outcome?

→ Is my attention appropriate?

→ Are my decisions purposeful?

→ Does my performance produce desired results?

→ Adjust as needed.

Let's review the other performance variables.

# ACTION

Many people are wrong when they think about improving their performance. They believe action is the key variable. Like Nike used to say, "Just Do It." This puts the emphasis on action. For example, I want to run faster, so I will run faster. But, as you now know, it doesn't work like that.

Our actions are either voluntary—our brain decides to act—or involuntarily—our body decides to act. Essentially, this variable is always controlled by the mind, consciously or subconsciously. While our conscious actions are driven by decisions, which we covered in depth, a lot of our subconscious actions are driven by "hardwired" decisions over time that form patterns—habitual behaviors. Habits are very important to recognize and analyze because they provide insights into your strengths and weaknesses that may stem from subconscious decisions, cognitive biases, and addictions that are preventing you from being your best.

After making a decision to act, the important part comes in—*evaluation of your action*. You need to determine whether your decision will drive the necessary performance to produce the desired result. The evaluation process provides the ability to create a continuous improvement loop that will allow you to learn from the past (so you can improve in the future). Ultimately, this improves your ability to perform to reach your goals, helping to reduce failure and maximize success.

# ABILITY

When it comes to your ability, there are many factors to evaluate when you want to get better using the Purpose First Performance Equation. We discussed your abilities in Chapter 2. Moving forward, I encourage you to focus on the time, resources, and energy it takes to improve your abilities compared to the level of improvement and the impact it will have on reaching your goal.

Below is a short list of your abilities to consider; however, this is not meant to be an exclusive list.

- **Creativity:** your ability to generate or recognize ideas, alternatives, or possibilities that may be beneficial
- **Emotional intelligence:** your ability to understand, use, and manage your own emotions in positive ways
- **Intelligence:** your ability to think, learn, and act according to a situation and the circumstances
- **Knowledge:** your familiarity with, awareness of, or understanding of someone or something
- **Physical ability:** your ability to perform an activity that requires physical characteristics such as strength, stamina, flexibility, coordination, etc.
- **Skills:** your expertise or talent needed to do a job or task

Once you analyze your abilities, think about how you rank. What are your physical, mental, and emotional strengths and weaknesses? Where do you have the most experience, skills, and competencies?

How can you build on what you do well to accelerate reaching your goal? Where are your gaps? Can you fill the gaps with support from others to complement your weaknesses so you can focus on what you do well?

After you've thought these things through, rank the top areas that you need to develop and start with those. You should now have a good idea of the abilities needed to reach your goal and how to develop a plan to maximize them. Bottom line, your self-awareness and self-management around your strengths and weaknesses is critical to your success.

# CIRCUMSTANCE

When it comes to maximizing your results, altering your circumstances may yield the most impressive outcomes. It also explains why so many people with the same abilities yield vastly different results.

Your circumstances often play an enormous part in your success, or lack thereof. Ask yourself, *Am I in the best position to perform at my best given my natural abilities and the circumstances I need to use them?* What are the current circumstances that impact your performance? Are they advantages or disadvantages? What are clear obstacles that prevent you from reaching your goals or slow you down? List them. What is controllable? What is uncontrollable, and how does it affect both your life and your profession?

This is what we are going to explore in the next chapter.

meaningful impact on your circumstances. As I stated, there are differences from country to country, state to state, and in many cities, it can even be block to block. Often where you live within a city makes a huge difference in the number of obstacles that you need to overcome to have an equal playing field, which often depends on your economic situation.

To help highlight the impact of where you're born, and its impact on an entrepreneur's path to success, let's look at the approximately 650,000 individuals known as Dreamers, who were brought to the United States as children and have lived here since. Seventy-four percent were born in Mexico or Central America, eleven percent are from the Caribbean and South America, nine percent from Asia, and six percent are from other areas in the rest of the world.

These individuals didn't make the decision to come to the United States. They were brought here by their parents. They are now, on average, in their mid-twenties, with the oldest being in their late thirties. They are hardworking, educated, law-abiding individuals. They are in school or have graduated from high school and college, have served in the armed forces, and do not pose a threat to national security or public safety. They have done nothing wrong. However, their circumstances are in the hands of our government's shifting laws and policies, driven by political forces.

Recently, the Supreme Court offered the Dreamers new hope, ensuring that their circumstances regarding where they live, learn, and work wouldn't be completely upended. On June 18, 2020, the Supreme Court rejected the Trump administration's attempt to end the Deferred Action for Childhood Arrivals (DACA) program, which allows qualified DACA enrollees to work, study, and remain in the United States on a renewable permit.

The Court's five-to-four decision shows how the Dreamers' circumstances could have changed in a second. Quoting the respondents in the case in the majority opinion he authored, Chief Justice John Roberts acknowledged, "Since 2012, DACA recipients have 'enrolled in degree programs, embarked on careers, started businesses, purchased homes, and even married and had children.'"[18]

If the decision was four to five, it wouldn't matter whether you were the best in your class, school, or profession. Your circumstances would abruptly change. You would be deported, ending your degree, career, business, and life as you knew it. These Dreamers are resilient and continue to work through these circumstances, but it provides perspective on how all the variables in the Purpose First Performance Equation, and in this case, your circumstances, impact your ability to reach your goals.

## HOW MUCH MONEY YOU HAVE

An entrepreneur's socioeconomic circumstances also will contribute to the ease or difficulty in building their business as well. If they are born into a wealthy or poor family, it will make a huge difference. If their father or mother is the CEO of a Fortune 500 company in London, or the top lawyer at a prestigious law firm in New York City, they will likely have different opportunities presented to them than the son or daughter of a maintenance worker in Hammond, Indiana or of a dental hygienist out of Victoria, Texas.

Access to education will also be an advantage or disadvantage to these entrepreneurs, depending on socioeconomic status. Not to mention, the role of family, friends, and affiliated networks that shapes access to critical knowledge, helpful connections, and venture capital. These socioeconomic circumstances often are combined with other factors, such as race, to tilt the playing field in favor of or against an entrepreneur.

## WHAT YOU LOOK LIKE

Race makes a huge difference because it is so visible—literally black or white, or any other skin tone associated with a legacy of bias that can impact an entrepreneur's circumstances. The cultural awareness of conscious and unconscious bias against people of color reached a new high with the murder of George Floyd. The outpouring of support to permanently change the systems that promote hate, racism, and inequality gives us hope these biases will be eradicated. However, for the entrepreneurs of color, those changes still impact their ability to perform at their best. Their circumstances are impacted simply by the color of their skin.

I got a good perspective on this from Garry Cooper, the founder and CEO of Rheaply, a platform that makes it easy for organizations to sell, exchange, and manage assets. As an African American, Garry is also familiar with the challenges and discomfort of being one of the few black students (and sometimes the only black student) in university-level science programs and being an entrepreneur. He received his PhD in Neuroscience from Northwestern University in 2014 and went on to complete a postdoctoral fellowship through Northwestern's Feinberg School of Medicine. Now he considers it a passion to make himself visible and available to other aspiring scientists and entrepreneurs of color.

Here's how Garry explains it,

Starting a business is hard. Most first-time founders take the leap because they have a pretty good idea: a better product, an improved business model, or key insights that the existing market has left unaddressed. Thinking, 'There has to be a better way,' is a common prelude to an entity's eventual creation.

But then reality hits. A new business and its first-time founders have to build, market, and sell a product or service that probably competes directly with existing offerings. Early market traction, specifically in business-to-business start-ups, is contingent on more than just superior marketing and the quality of the product or service. It is many times primarily based on establishing relationships with key customers to facilitate adoption and growth.

Now, imagine you're a racial minority and starting your first enterprise business.

This venture might enjoy some advantages: a great early product offering, firsthand insights into customer needs, and a hardworking brain trust. But, undoubtedly, this founder will not have an established set of potential early customers or a sufficient personal network to easily drive business. The central reasons for this vary, but historic and systemic racial discrepancies in business ownership, corporate leadership, and finance continue to hinder progress for minority founders. One need not look further than the disproportionate differences between the African American population (13.4%) and their representation in the business world (only four Fortune 500 companies have black chief executives).[19]

When we peel this back to better understand why, we can use the Purpose First Performance Equation to understand it in more detail. It can't be explained by just a lack of ability or purpose or subpar decisions. From a big-picture perspective, it is logical to look at a systemic flaw in circumstances or, simply put, a permanently unlevel playing field. This is undeniable if you look back in history.

## HOW YOU IDENTIFY

Just like race, the gender you identify with impacts your circumstances as well. Women's rights are still denied throughout the world. In many countries in the Middle East, women must get permission to even get a job, let alone start a business. Although women in the United States have more rights, biases still exist, whether they are spoken or unspoken. Hell, it took the Mississippi legislature 64 years to vote in 1984 and ratify the 19th Amendment, acknowledging that women were fully enfranchised citizens.

These biases have an impact on the circumstances of a female entrepreneur, which impacts the playing field on which they are trying to perform at their best. The biases are even more overt and destructive for people whose gender identity doesn't align with social norms. Keep in mind, gender identity is the personal sense of one's own gender. It can correlate with a person's assigned sex at birth or can differ from it. Their personal ability to successfully start a business is frequently compromised by the laws in the city or state in which they operate their business, which clearly demonstrates a direct correlation between individual circumstances and overall performance.

Although these biases create an unfair playing field, laws that protect and enforce them show how difficult it is for some people to succeed as entrepreneurs. The Purpose First Performance Equation can demonstrate this is true and can help people understand the impact of their circumstances on their performance and their capacity to reach their goals.

It is important that each of us is fighting to ensure equality. You can also see the impact. On June 15, 2020, the Supreme Court ruled that federal civil rights law protects gay, lesbian, and transgender workers. The landmark ruling extended protections to millions of workers nationwide and was a defeat for the Trump administration, which argued that Title VII of the Civil Rights Act, which bars discrimination based on sex, did not extend to claims of gender identity and sexual orientation.

The majority opinion was written by Justice Neil Gorsuch, who was joined by Chief Justice John Roberts and the Court's four liberal justices. Gorsuch wrote:

> An employer who fires an individual for being homosexual or transgender fires that person for traits or actions it would not have questioned in members of a different sex. Sex plays a necessary and undisguisable role in the decision, exactly what Title VII forbids.[20]

This ruling shows the power of institutions. Fortunately, this decision is one of the Court's most significant rulings ever with respect to the civil rights of gay and transgender individuals in the workplace, but it creates a host of other challenges to discrimination on the basis of sexual orientation or transgender status.

President Joe Biden said it well: "The Supreme Court has confirmed the simple but profoundly American idea that every human being should be treated with respect and dignity. That everyone should be able to live openly, proudly, as their true selves, without fear."[21]

The right to live and work without systemic oppression should be a value every entrepreneur should champion. We want to allow entrepreneurs to be successful on the merits of their businesses and their abilities, not be held back by their race, sex, or orientation.

This ruling helped to take one major step forward for the LGBTQ community, which is made up of approximately 1 million workers who identify as transgender and 7.1 million lesbian, gay, and bisexual workers, according to UCLA's Williams Institute.[22] A number of LGBTQ groups rightfully celebrated the Court's ruling, including the Human Rights Campaign, whose president, Alphonso David, said in a tweet that the decision is a "landmark victory for #LGBTQ equality."[23]

It is the concept of equality that creates a level playing field for all of us to play on, fairly!

As outlined, there are many uncontrollable factors that define an entrepreneur's circumstances, making it easier or harder for them to reach their goals. As you reflect on your circumstances and how they impact your performance, it's easy to understand the importance of equality. Without equality, we systemically provide advantages to those who control the circumstances. The ironic element is that those who have the most power to change the rules are the most likely to be disadvantaged by doing so. However, for those with power and Purpose Pillars affiliated with justice and fairness, we accept this challenge.

# WHAT YOU BELIEVE IN

Many Purpose Pillars are anchored by people's spirituality. I was baptized in the Catholic Church. I had no control over that decision, given it happened when I was an infant. As I grew up, my religious beliefs, which were central to my family's value system, were a big part of my perspective on the world. They shaped my circumstances by establishing what was right, wrong, acceptable, unacceptable, possible, and impossible. Although I wouldn't go to jail for missing church on Sunday, my failure to attend was unacceptable to my family and the church. Ultimately, I would go because I knew this was what was expected of me to stay in the good graces of my parents and the priests and nuns I interacted with. This is just a small example of how these institutions influence your behaviors. But it gets a lot more complicated.

Religions unite people under common gods, spiritual beliefs, and value systems. Many people's Purpose Pillars include their faith. They are deeply connected to their spirituality, and it is something they will defend to the death. This unwavering and deeply instilled perspective on the world, based on their religion, shapes their personal circumstances throughout life. It provides a foundation that guides life decisions, often from birth, since their families' views and values are grounded in it. The best of these values are based on justice, kindness, and hope.

Over the centuries, these beliefs were galvanized into religious institutions. Over time, leaders of these institutions have been aligned with and in conflict with secular institutions, such as business, military, and government. Like-minded leaders have created advantages that have benefited certain religions while persecuting others. Based on the religion you practice, you may not be recognized by the country in which you were born, or worse, you may be killed by the leaders of that country because of your religion. These laws completely change circumstances and potential for success because of where you live and the religion that you practice. The right to decide what religion you want to practice is essential to freedom. Therefore, people will die defending their faith and their right to choose.

What happens if the religion you practice does not support your right to marry, even though the law of the land does? Ironic, right? Although, we do have a choice of the faith we practice in America, this decision will impact your circumstances. For example, what if the religion that you grew up with doesn't support your view of equality and justice as an adult? Perhaps the religion doesn't allow women to hold top leadership positions. Does your choice to continue to practice that religion influence your view of equality in your start-up, even, perhaps, subconsciously? It is likely—and very human—that those subconscious thoughts influence your view of diversity, equity, and inclusion in your business. As a result, they will shape your circumstances.

However, you do have a choice about what religion you practice, especially in the United States. The religion you practice early in your life may not be in your control, but over time, we do gain control of of that choice. This is a great example of a big decision you are capable of making to change your circumstance in life and work. Deciding to practice another religion aligned with your Purpose Pillars is a very viable option that is likely to help harmonize your values with your day-to-day actions. Or another decision might lead to the change you want in the institution you are a part of so it aligns with your values and changes the systems for others that follow you. Or you might do nothing. You have the power to change your circumstances with your decisions.

# WHO YOUR FAMILY AND FRIENDS ARE

Other circumstances may seem unchangeable, like, for example, your family. And they are. Well, sort of. To illustrate my point, I'll tell you that I was born into a family of three boys and three girls. Those are my siblings. Forever. That goes for my parents, grandparents, aunts, and cousins. I was not able to pick them literally (uncontrollable), but I was able to decide how they will influence my life (controllable).

Often our family is the source of our most enduring values, a provider of powerful unconditional love, and the cornerstone for who we are as people. Building healthy, enduring relationships with your family may be one of your Purpose Pillars. Healthy family relationships help you to perform at your best. Although challenging at times, your family helps you feel connected, nurtured, and loved. They challenge you to be your best and are there to celebrate your success. They also offer a shoulder to cry on and a hand to help you up if you fail. They provide powerful emotional support so essential to humans, which helps create the right circumstances for us to succeed. We want to foster these relationships that allow us to be ourselves and help us be our best.

But sometimes family relationships can be toxic and very unhealthy. Getting support to help exit mentally and physically abusive relationships is essential. Although very difficult for a variety of reasons, this is critical for your physical and emotional safety. Many people endure a lifetime of unhealthy relationships with family members or overall toxic family environments that might not be as overt or acute. The never-ending experience robs them of their self-worth, purpose, and hope. Often you don't even recognize the destructive nature because it is all you know. Or maybe you want to fix it, but neither party knows how. Or you recognize it and want to fix it, but the desire to repair it is not reciprocated.

The ideas of familial toxicity or positivity can also extend to your friendships. While you get to choose your friends (controllable), often, many friendships can feel like family—so much so, that we sometimes overlook bad influences, toxic exchanges, or reactive, comparative friendships that we may have outgrown but don't know how to address. We may feel we owe it to our friends to maintain our relationship because of our history together, when, in fact, if you walk away from your time together and feel drained, exhausted, annoyed, or saddened, it might be time for a serious evaluation.

Regardless, it can be a difficult environment to break free from. However, once recognized, you need to change your family or friend dynamics to free yourself so you can be your best. You can often get support from family counselors or mental health professionals to help take the appropriate steps to give you back control of your life without *being* controlled. By taking steps to nurture healthy family and friend relationships—even if the best step is to terminate the relationship—you will eventually create a more optimal circumstance for your happiness and success.

# CONTROL THE UNCONTROLLABLE

We spend so much time trying to change ourselves, we sometimes forget to focus on changing our circumstances—an important Purpose First Performance Equation variable that matters so much. I tried to highlight how circumstance impacts your performance. As I pointed out, many of those circumstances are out of your control (e.g., birthplace) and have a major impact on your ability to be successful. Some of them may *seem* uncontrollable but are based on your decisions to change them (e.g., religion).

Heck, some of the circumstances you face that impact you may motivate you to change them. It may become your Purpose Vision, such as changing a law or a system that discriminates against a certain population of people. It may even become the focus of your Purpose First Business. Nevertheless, I believe it illuminates the impact of circumstance on your work and life.

In any case, by now you should have a pretty good idea of how uncontrollable circumstances impact your business and life. Depending on who you are and what circumstances are engulfing you, it may benefit you or limit your ability to perform. Once you are aware of how your circumstances are negatively impacting your performance, you must do everything you can to alter them.

On the flip side, there are many aspects you do control that can improve your circumstance and get better results. To help frame the concept, let me say that a Purpose First Entrepreneur has a lot of power. You control a lot of the variables in the Purpose First Performance Equation. You actually control a lot more than the average person, because you are the helm of a new venture, which is truly a blank slate. Although you may have a lack of control as an employee at another business, as an entrepreneur, you get to hit the reset button on a host of important factors that will contribute to your lack of success.

Below, you'll get a sense of the decisions that will impact your circumstances and ultimately your success:

- What type of business will you operate? (Business Model)
- Where will you open your office(s)? (Location)
- What do you do to build the business? (Role)
- Who will you recruit to help build the business? (Team)
- What are the formal policies for business behavior? (Rules)
- How does your organization behave? (Culture)

This is not meant to be an all-inclusive list. There are many circumstances you can control and influence. Like a pilot flying with strong tailwinds, an entrepreneur making the right decisions to improve their circumstances will have the wind at her back, accelerating her path to success.

## OPTIMIZE YOUR CIRCUMSTANCES

Let's explore the list above. Selecting an industry that is rapidly expanding will make it easier to be successful than building a business in an industry that is contracting. Think brick-and-mortar retail versus online retail. Your online store could be up running in no time with turnkey solutions like SquareSpace (e-commerce website), ActiveCampaign (customer experience software), and

ShipBob (fulfillment). Your cost would be low and your flexibility high, and your customer access would be unlimited. However, setting up a traditional storefront would be expensive and customer access would be mostly local. Both are retail businesses, but e-commerce is rapidly expanding while brick-and-mortar businesses are shrinking.

Another example of the same industry with different models would be the news. Let's say you want to focus on being the source for "good news" about equality in America. If you decide to print a newspaper, your cost would be significantly higher than sending it out digitally. Same with your content. Do you hire your own writers or use artificial intelligence to aggregate relevant content from almost unlimited sources?

These are important decisions that impact your circumstances. If you decide you and two of your friends will write all of the content, you have created a different model than if you'd used AI technology to find the best stories. Although both companies are in the news business, the overall circumstances in which they operate will be very different.

Where you start your company will impact a lot of factors—for example, your access to talent, capital, and tax incentives. The quality of life for employees and their costs to live will be impacted by your decisions. It is rare for entrepreneurs to create a list of pros and cons for where they are starting a business, but why not? This may be one of the biggest factors for creating optimal circumstances for your business's performance.

It may also be the time to reevaluate your need for a centralized workforce altogether. The global pandemic forced workers to go remote. People saw an increase in productivity and high job satis-faction ratings, resulting in many companies allowing employees to work remotely permanently. This trend will certainly help many entrepreneurs keep their costs down while still attracting global talent. It may even accelerate market penetration because you can deploy clusters of employees in multiple cities that are a part of your roll-out strategy.

Your role in your company will most likely have the biggest impact on your circumstances. It might make sense that, since you came up with the idea and started the company, you should be the CEO. Right? It's kind of like if you wrote a great script, which means you should be the lead actor. At first, it might make sense. Well, kind of. In the beginning, you will probably be the only person who really understands how the main character should think and feel and who can fully express the desired story arc.

So you take the lead role. You get your friends at the local theater group to join the cast. They love the script. They are tremendously excited about what it could be. After a lot of tireless hours of rehearsal, you finally unveil the play to your first audience. For the most part, everybody likes it. However, it doesn't really turn out the way you and the cast thought it would. The reality is, you're a very average actor who wrote a great play. Does that mean your play can't be sensational? No. You just need to have the right people in the right roles, which means you probably shouldn't be the lead actor.

This is very similar to the decision you'll face as a founder. You came up with the idea, sure. You recruited an enthusiastic team to help you build your product. It's good but has a lot of unmet potential. You have to really evaluate whether you are in the right role to build a great company. The role of CEO may make sense at first, but you have to keep evaluating it as your company grows. Regardless of your decisions, it will have a tremendous impact on the circumstances you create for your business to meet its potential.

Your company will be defined by your role. However, it will be shaped more in the long run by the people and culture you put in place. They have a huge influence on creating the right circumstances for the company to succeed. A Purpose First Entrepreneur will create the best environment for success by being very purposeful about both. By establishing your company's Purpose Vision and Purpose Pillars at the beginning, you will make intentional choices to ensure you create the right foundation.

Often entrepreneurs are so excited about the business they are creating, they are immersed in activity. They're not thinking about company culture. It's probably just a couple of people, so it's an afterthought. However, by the time you realize your culture is suboptimal, it's too late. Or certainly, hard to change. By focusing on the culture around your company's purpose and Purpose Pillars, you establish a framework for a powerful culture.

You will create the best circumstances for a world-class culture if you start building it from day one. This will allow you to hire the right people from the beginning. Those people will help you strengthen it and help it evolve to get better and better. The more you develop the right culture by rewarding people for fostering it and eliminating people that harm it, the more likely you are to create the right circumstances for success.

You may make all the right decisions to create the best circumstances to reach your goal, and it all can change in an instant. Something that you had no control of, such as a global pandemic, may abruptly disrupt or destroy everything you worked for. These events can be catastrophic, such as a tornado, or can be life threatening, like cancer, or emotionally debilitating, like the death of a loved one. Though, keep in mind, not all uncontrollable events are bad (such as winning the lottery or getting stuck in an elevator with your future significant other).

These events may transform our lives, for better or worse. They may accelerate our paths to success. However, they may slow or stop our progress or deflate us as well. Maybe so much so, we stop trying. When things get bad, that is when our Purpose Pillars can support us. If we nurture them along the way, we can return to them at any point we feel lost.

After I got hit in the head, my brain swelled so much, they couldn't insert a plate in my skull to replace the bone that was crushed from the force of the club. Once the swelling went down, I went back in for my second surgery to put the plate in. After the surgery, I finally got the energy to go to the bathroom on my own. As I walked into the bathroom, the mirror reflected an emaciated teenager with a shaved head and big stitches running from the front to the back. It was gruesome. I thought, *Why me?*

*What did I do to deserve this? This is not fair! I deserve a freaking break after my parents dying when I was a kid. I did everything that I was supposed to do. Now I can barely function as a human being, and I look like Frankenstein!*

I just started crying. I thought about everything that I was supposed to be that I could no longer be. I wasn't going to play college football anymore. Hell, I wasn't even sure I was going to be able to read or write again. While I certainly couldn't control my parents dying or my being violently attacked, these circumstances altered my future immeasurably. I was able to recover physically, mentally, and emotionally, and forge a different path. My experience made me stronger and helped me be the best I can be right now.

Honestly, it took a while to develop this Purpose First Mindset. However, it allowed me to really reflect on the fact that the world is often uncontrollable, but we control much more than we think. We control what is important to us, we control how we behave, and we control the goals we set. We can't guarantee success, but we can commit to the pursuit of being our best selves. The Purpose First Performance Equation helps you focus on what matters to you while enjoying the journey in the pursuit of what matters to you.

Now, prioritize what changes you can make in your circumstances to accelerate hitting your goals. And create the plan to get there.

# CHAPTER 9

# THE POWER OF PURPOSEFUL DECISION-MAKING

Becoming the best Purpose First Entrepreneur you can be will ultimately be reached one purposeful decision at a time. However, many of your decisions are made on the fly in the heat of the moment, or they come with endless agonizing, weighing options, worry, and chatting about it nonstop. Anxiety about making decisions often prevents the decision itself. These barriers that prevent you from making good decisions need to be removed.

If you want to perform at an elite level, your decisions need to be purposeful—meaning both on-purpose and purpose driven.

Let's set the stage… Say your goal is to create your own creative design business, but things aren't going as planned. Your first client wants the first project for free, but if you give it to them, you set the precedent that your time and work isn't worth anything.

If you make the wrong decision, your first client may walk. Instead of weighing pros and cons to an obsessive degree, simply pause. Ask yourself, *Is my attention focused on this specific decision?* Most likely there is a lot of "noise in your head." It may come from past decisions like this that didn't turn out, or the unhelpful imaginary voice of your friends telling you never to trust clients because they are all sneaky. Regardless, become mindful you are making a decision.

Once your attention is appropriate, ask yourself, *What is truly my* desired outcome? *What's my end goal?* In this case, you weigh several factors: (1) not getting paid, (2) lack of value for work, (3) opportunity to close the first client, (4) opportunity to use this client as reference to get new clients, and (5) the precedent that the first project is free for all future clients.

Upon mindful reflection, you decide that your time and work is too important to you to give it away for free. By agreeing to do your first project for free, you are not validating your business model. You want to know people will pay you for your creative design as a stand-alone business. In addition, if you use the client as a reference, he may tell the prospective client to ask for a free first project too. Basically, you would be creating your own recurring problem. It might be different if your product were software, but your time isn't scalable as such.

So you tell your prospective first client that you understand his position; however, this project, if done right, will be extremely beneficial to his business. Therefore, you both agree there is value if the project is done well. And since you are creating the design, there is value in your work that you want to be paid for. You understand the client may be apprehensive about becoming your first client, despite the fact that you've been doing this professionally for a larger firm, so you will offset the risk by providing a money-back guarantee.

This decision is very purposeful. It aligns with your desired outcome: to validate your business model. It prompts the client to make a decision that if he values your work enough, he should pay you for it. However, it makes the decision less risky for the client by providing a money-back guarantee. Furthermore, you realize that if the client wants his money back after the project, it wouldn't be a good reference anyway. And it will help you evaluate your performance, thus addressing your primary goal of validating yourself—can you quit your day job and start your business? Or do you need to adjust your approach by setting clear client expectations from the start?

# MAKE BETTER DECISIONS

The more purposeful your decisions, the more successful you will be. Therefore, I recommend establishing a decision tree to help you make good decisions more routinely. The **Purpose First Decision Tree** I shared in Chapter 7 can guide you through the process, to help you get what you really want, but more specifically, show you *how* to make decisions get what you really want. Going through each question will prompt you to calibrate your attention and be more purposeful. This allows you to be more intentional about decisions. It helps you focus on the goal of the decision, or more specifically, your true desired result of the decision.

Once you know you are making a decision, you are in a better place to make a more purposeful decision. One that is intentional. One that is aligned with your Purpose Vision and Purpose Pillars and goals. Giving the appropriate attention to decisions gives you a new power to make *better* and more purposeful choices. Decisions dictate how we perform and the results we get.

After making the decision, the important part comes in. Evaluate whether your decision and performance produced the desired result. This may be the most important part of the process because the evaluation provides the ability to create a continuous improvement loop that will allow you to learn from the past (so you can improve the future). Ultimately, this improves your decision-making abilities, which reduces failure and maximizes success.

# GET IN THE ZONE

Mindfulness upgrades your ability to make purposeful decisions. Author and psychologist Dan Mager provides a very practical way to understand mindfulness by comparing the human body to a computer operating system. If the human body's OS is the brain and nervous system, then, according to Mager,

> Mindfulness can upgrade your internal operating system by helping to make the unconscious conscious and create the space for reasoned and skillful responses, even in the face of highly charged feelings...
>
> Mindfulness can help you better tolerate and stay with difficult emotions, so they don't hold you hostage. You can increase your ability to bear discomfort—physically and emotionally—and be present with it, without being suffocated by it or needing to push it away. When you enlarge your capacity to bear emotional discomfort, you are less likely to react automatically to your emotions or let them control you.[24]

Mindfulness allows you to create powerful gaps between a stimulus and response. Strengthening your ability to do this consistently will be game-changing for you, because it allows you to make purposeful decisions, which is at the heart of maximizing your performance.

To make purposeful decisions, you must be mindful.

If you are alive and well in today's world, you know being mindful is really tough. We battle constant interruptions that take us away from proper workflow, tasks, family, and even sleep. It's no longer unusual to be out to dinner while checking your phone, or to be in a meeting while working, texting, and attempting to hold a conversation. While we can multitask, our brains are not made to multi-focus.

You need to retrain your brain to make better decisions. We've all heard of being "in the zone." Whether it's work, sports, or music, you know what it feels like to be so engaged, time flies and you feel unstoppable. However, this "zone" mentality can feel fleeting. Even so, with practice, it is possible to tap into it on a regular basis.

The **Purpose First Mindset** provides the framework for getting the optimal decision-making *zone*. It is anchored by your purpose with three key supporting elements: your *focus*, your *awareness*, and your *state of mind*.

## Purpose First Mindset

- **Focus**: You cut through the noise—chaos, obstacles, doubt—to align with your purpose and your Purpose Pillars. You focus on what matters to you and execute on your planned strategies to reach your goals.
- **Awareness**: You are mindful in the moment, which allows you to also be aware of what is around you and what is emerging. As a result, you may seize on a new approach that is better for reaching your goals than what was planned.
- **State of Mind**: You are cognizant of thoughts that are affecting your ability to accurately assess reality. Your thoughts may be influenced by bias, previous failures, unmet desires, etc. Being mindful helps optimize your state of mind. It reduces the noise

that swirls around in your head, which improves your decision-making.

So what happens when all three elements are in harmony? You're in the **Purpose First Mindset Zone**—the perfect position to make great decisions.

Being in the zone should be reserved for Type A people alone, right?

Not even close.

Achieving the Purpose First Mindset Zone is not about perfection. It's about aligning with your purpose and performing your best to achieve your goals. Any person can live purposefully and in the zone on a daily basis. It all starts with mental preparedness and knowing your desired outcome. You have to possess a balance of focus, awareness, and state of mind, and apply it to how you make purposeful decisions.

Let me give you a non-work-related example that I think will drive this point home.

When I do high-intensity interval training (HIIT) workouts at the gym, I start off with a clear, desired outcome. I want to make sure I maximize my overall heart fitness. I don't walk into the gym without a plan. I have specific target heart rate zones I want to hit. With performance technology like WHOOP or fitness studio apps like Orangetheory, it is easy to measure and manage all of this. However, it is not always easy to achieve it.

So how do I make sure to reach my desired outcome? Usually, I start with a clear *focus* on my goal. About a quarter of the way through the workout, I become *aware* that my legs are starting to burn, and it feels like my heart is going to explode. My *state of mind* slips downward. I start thinking about why it might not be a good day to work so hard—I didn't sleep well, my knee kind of hurts, blah, blah, blah—and I start to reflexively slow down. Then, I look at my app. I see my heart rate drop from the top zone to a lower zone. Yikes!

Then I remind myself of the *purpose* for being there, and I refocus on my workout goal. As a result, my focus, awareness, and state of mind recalibrate. My *focus* sharpens. I start pushing harder. I am no longer *aware* of my burning muscles and racing heart; however, I am *aware* of how I feel. I'm in the *zone*. My body is going full out, and as a result, my *state of mind* refreshes; I feel completely alive.

So, while this is great for exercise, how does it translate to work? I'll tell you. It all comes back to being in a Purpose First Mindset. Often in high-stakes meetings, things can get crazy. During those times, I pause, make sure I'm mindful, and ask myself one question: *Is my attention appropriate?* "Appropriate?" you might ask. "What does that even mean?" This concept is really broken down into three questions.

- **Am I focused?** Determine whether you are aligned with your purpose, are focused on your goal, and have a clear plan to achieve your desired outcome. Don't let your focus on your goals get hijacked.
- **Am I aware?** Be aware of any new information that might diverge from your original strategy but will optimize your path to your desired outcome. Sometimes we get so focused on our original strategy that we can't see an opportunity that's literally right in front of us. But this new opportunity might not be part of the previous plan, so we ignore it. However, if you stay aware, you will recognize that the "new" way can be a better way (or not) to achieve your desired outcome. It just takes awareness.
- **What is my state of mind?** Evaluate your emotional state of mind. We are often influenced by emotion: fear, anger, doubt, anxiety, etc. Assess how those emotions cloud your ability to focus on the desired outcomes, especially when you are emotionally triggered. Make good decisions based on facts, not emotions.

This simple question—*Is my attention appropriate?*—usually resets my attention and helps me make decisions when I'm in the zone or trying to get there. Then, *focus on your desired outcome*. Like with any goal, we may get caught up in the process. The minutiae. The drama. The setbacks or failures. Keep your eye on the desired outcome. Define your ultimate goal for the day. For your workout. For how you want to feel.

Focus on one thing at a time—one goal, one outcome—to intentionally stay in the zone and achieve what you set out to do. Don't talk yourself down. We are conditioned to have a "fight-or-flight" response. It's so easy to back down when things get tough. This is especially true when it's a physical feat, but even more so when you are wavering in your start-up life. Visualize what you want, and then go after it without talking yourself out of it.

Let's put this all into context for Purpose First Entrepreneurs by examining how to use the Purpose First Decision Tree and the Purpose First Mindset in the real world.

Most entrepreneurs are exceptional at thinking big. They can picture what success looks like more easily than most people. Right? Why else would they put themselves through the painful process of building a company? Keep in mind, everyone is telling them it will be hard, and there is plenty of evidence that those naysayers are right. So how do they achieve it?

Many times, the start is the easiest because everything is new. It's kind of like a marathon. You've prepared to run the race— just as an entrepreneur does a lot of prep—and now you're at the starting line. The first few miles or so are pretty easy, or at least, as expected. But it's the messy middle that can be difficult. It's mile fifteen when you start to really feel it—similar to how an entrepreneur feels after the first fifteen months.

Like a marathoner "feels it," the entrepreneur also feels the impact of building the business—mentally, physically, and emotionally. The deals that didn't close, the features in the app that the customers didn't like, the employees that didn't pan out. Your mental state is worn down. Your desired outcome is still clear— to finish the marathon—but you're starting to pay more attention to the burn in your muscles and predicting the challenges you'll face the next 11.2 miles or so. Can you make it? You're not as optimistic as you were during mile one or two, or even five.

Now is the time when you need to take a personal inventory: what do you have to do to achieve your goal? You can slow down your pace, you can pace yourself off another runner, or you can walk at the next water stop to recalibrate. There are a host of options available to you. You weren't thinking about this at the start of the race, but you need to think about it now to achieve your goal. In other words, these are emergent opportunities you can follow that are different from your original plan, but they will help you get to the same desired outcome: finishing the marathon, something only about 0.05% of the US population does each year.[25]

This is the same challenge you will be faced with as an entrepreneur. You build your start-up according to a business plan. As things start to roll out, your plan needs to be adjusted. You ask yourself, *Is my goal to build a successful start-up?* If yes, then you have to ask yourself, *How do I achieve that goal given my current state?* It's not about where you hoped you would be in 15 months, but where you are now that you are *at* 15 months.

Get your head right. Get in the current state. Now that you are there, evaluate what your options are. Don't get bogged down by the fact that someone told you 12 months ago to do something that you didn't do but need to do now. Don't get hung up on trying to right a wrong. Instead, get focused on taking the action needed to achieve your goals now that this path is the best option. Don't let your ego prevent you from taking that option. Recalibrate to your current state. If the best option is to narrow your focus on a specific target market to maximize your usage and minimize your burn, then do it.

# A PURPOSE FIRST CASE STUDY

Here's a good example of a company that didn't get consumed in what they were supposed to be. They took advantage of what they could be.

The company is Packback.

I met one of the Packback co-founders, Mike Shannon, in an elevator (it was literally and figuratively an elevator pitch). He was telling me, in his very matter-of-fact style, about how the company was going to transform the way professors selected college textbooks and students bought them (much more affordably). They were creating a better product that cost less.

I was intrigued. I wasn't the only one. A few months later, on March 21, 2014, Packback appeared on ABC's *Shark Tank*. Mike and co-founder Kasey Gandham left as winners with a $250,000 investment from Mark Cuban in exchange for 20% equity (and a few good laughs). Shortly after, there was a formal investment round that my firm was a part of. We were confident that Packback was going to transform the college book market and, eventually, books as we know them.

Fast-forward to today: Packback hasn't sold *one* college textbook all year. #BustNotReally Through the leadership of Mike and Kasey and the other co-founders, Nick Currier and Jessica Tenuta, the business changed direction. They didn't get hung up on focusing on the original business model that they spent years building. They captured a unique opportunity to evolve their model to what the users really needed and wanted, which is a more effective way for students to learn by optimizing how they engage with professors and other students.

Packback is now an AI-supported online discussion platform that enables curiosity-based student discussion. And they are rocking it! Universities love it. Professors love it. Students really love it! And everyone is loving it even more as an increasing number of classes moved online during the pandemic. As a result of being aware, Packback is in a much better position to solve real problems for students everywhere.

In the start-up world, many people would call this a "pivot." The idea of changing direction to align your business with emergent opportunities. The pivot is core to my point. You are aware of your desired outcome. The current situation (e.g., business growing slower than anticipated) doesn't match your "prediction" when you started (e.g., your business growing like Google did). However, your attention needs to be calibrated to be aware of the emergent opportunities available to you to develop a new plan to get you there.

Finally, in order to achieve this, you'll have to be strong enough to tell your ego to shut up. It's better to reach your goal than to never have to admit you weren't perfect. A lot of entrepreneurs get caught up here. And, unfortunately, they don't realize it until years pass and they reflect on their decisions.

Understanding how to be in a Purpose First Mindset and using the Purpose First Decision Tree will harness the power of your purpose and Purpose Pillars. These resources will retrain your brain to help you make better decisions and perform at elite level in all aspects of your life.

# CHAPTER 10

# THE START-UP ATHLETE

Entrepreneurs are like professional athletes. Top performance is critical to success. Therefore, it makes sense that we would have similar approaches to our mental and physical wellness, enabling us to perform at an elite level. However, many entrepreneurs do the opposite. They discount all the science about the importance of health in relation to job performance and grind themselves down to a point of mental and physical failure. How stupid is that?

Well, it takes one to know one. My wellness wakeup call came when I was lying helpless on an airport floor.

Feet shuffled around me. A bystander asked if I was all right, to which I responded, "I'm fine, I'm just resting," refusing to admit the truth of the matter. I was 37 at the time and had literally run myself into the ground.

I was at the helm of a growing company, working around the clock, consistently stressed, and putting my health low on the priority list. During this nonstop working lifestyle, I began to experience lower back pain that gradually worsened, but I told myself that I didn't have the time to take care of it. The pain intensified over the stretch of a couple of weeks to where I began having trouble getting out of bed in the morning and sitting at my desk for a prolonged period. Eventually, it hurt to move, period.

I was en route home to Chicago from Dallas when the final straw broke the camel's back (in this case, I was the camel). I could barely walk as I exited the cab and entered the airport. Once inside, I used the wall as a safety net. I eventually psyched myself up enough to push off the wall and hobble onward to the security checkpoint—resembling, I imagine, the Tin Man running out of oil.

It was at that moment, mid-stride, that my back gave out, and I collapsed. I laid flat out on the grimy airport floor, unable to move for what felt like minutes. I tried to roll over and help myself up, but I couldn't find the strength; finally, someone from the security staff came by to assist. Next thing, I was on a stretcher in an ambulance on my way to the emergency room. I stared with wide eyes at the ambulance ceiling, thinking, *What the hell am I doing to myself?*

I was treated at the hospital for a herniated disk that was pushing against my sciatic nerve. I was released from the emergency room and continued my journey home the next day, this time with a new outlook on my work, my life, and my health. I needed to make a change or face the consequences: declining health, limited function, and maybe even a stress-induced heart attack, if I wasn't careful.

Change didn't happen overnight. Instead, I took small steps that built on one another over time to produce an even better outcome than if I'd tried to completely overhaul everything at once. I started with a meditation practice after reading *The Relaxation Response* by Dr. Herbert Benson. Meditation allowed me to clear my mind, and with a clearer, healthier mind, my body followed suit. I had a newfound attitude around the mind-body connection and where my health really fit in it.

As my relationship with my health changed, and I became more in tune with my mind and body, I began to explore other outlets. I decided to incorporate group boxing classes into my routine. Group classes held me accountable and forced me to show up—I competed with no one but myself. As I felt myself getting stronger, I began to reflect on my diet and discovered ways to make that better, too. I committed to improving my diet so that I could perform better mentally and physically.

Next, I moved into strength training. Controlled, focused weight lifting had an enormous effect on my overall strength, my core, and my posterior chain—areas that I especially needed to work on after a back injury. I also began to measure my sleep. I looked at how my sleep affected my work and learned to optimize it, ultimately allowing me to perform at my best, day in and day out.

As you might imagine, as I took more time for myself and my health, I began to feel better physically, emotionally, and mentally. My life grew more satisfying, and I became a better, more productive entrepreneur.

I have since switched roles from entrepreneur to investor, but I still interact with countless entrepreneurs daily. And I've seen plenty of them run themselves into the ground, just as I did. For this reason, I've made it a personal mission to help other entrepreneurs and businesspeople get back on track by prioritizing their health. It's my goal to shift the conversation from the glamorization of overworking to the enormous benefits of taking time for personal wellness.

In fact, in 2019 I launched the Chicago Wellness Challenge, a six-week wellness program that calls on Chicago business leaders and entrepreneurs to engage, learn, and start moving toward their wellness goals. The Chicago Wellness Challenge was so powerful, I partnered with aSweatLife to roll out more programs in Chicago and other cities.

As I reflect on my wellness journey and that airport moment, as embarrassing as it was, I can't help but feel grateful for it. It was the wakeup call I needed. It not only changed my life for the better, but it also became a vehicle for helping me change the lives of others. Not to mention, the mental image of it still gives me a good laugh from time to time (what the hell was I thinking?!). It's sad, funny, and all too true.

## START-UP ATHLETE FUNDAMENTALS

# KNOW THE PLAYING FIELD

Building a start-up is a continuation of hard lessons learned. Sometimes, it seems like a continuous loop of Spartan Ultra Races. In other words, entrepreneurs feel that they are in a nonstop loop of ultramarathons with seemingly nonstop brutal obstacles that test their strength, endurance, and mental fortitude—every day, for years.

You will be challenged mentally, physically, and emotionally on a recurring basis. So you have to prepare yourself to not only survive, but thrive on the journey. If you take this seriously, you will be a better Purpose First Entrepreneur, directly aligning with the Wellness Purpose Pillar.

Think of it like you're a start-up athlete. You have to train to perform at your best.

You have to own your wellness. It must be a comprehensive and integrated approach because your physical health impacts your mental health, which impacts your emotional health. All of these elements are intertwined, so you have to be cognizant as you look for ways to improve.

To perform at your best, your mind and body need to be in shape. However, we live in a culture where everyone is looking for the fitness fad, the diet pill, or the quick fix to get healthy in the fastest way with minimal effort.

But wellness isn't just a number on a scale or physical aesthetics. It's more about overall wellness than outward appearances. So much of what we attribute to wellness is dictated by society's standards. Rarely do we ask ourselves what it means to be well, right? Maybe that doesn't mean going to a gym every day, eating a plant-based diet, or meditating for an hour each morning. Before you can *be* well, *you* have to *define wellness for you.*

And that starts here, with you.

In our go-go-go culture, people often work until they drop face-down on their desk. Go home and sleep for a couple of hours. Then they get up and do it all over again. While sometimes relentless persistence is absolutely necessary to get where you want to be, most can't afford to operate in that way consistently.

Performance will suffer. Your body will suffer. Your mind will suffer. Your relationships will suffer. Your overall health will suffer.

One of the biggest problems isn't that entrepreneurs' lives are more stressful as much as it is that their lives are so *continuously* stressful. Typically, entrepreneurs push themselves too hard without opportunities to recharge and improve physically, mentally, and emotionally. This pattern undermines long-term performance: in the office, at home, and everywhere in between.

When you combine continuous stress with a mostly sedentary lifestyle—addicted to screens and our chairs—a chain reaction of destruction begins to occur on a mental and physical level. High blood pressure, obesity, chronic illnesses, anger, and constant "buffering" to numb yourself to the pressures of life quickly replace any sort of in-depth examination of what you really need to feel better. In the absence of healthy relief from stress, many entrepreneurs seek easy and quick fixes to reduce the pressure by overeating, binge drinking, smoking, doing drugs, and other unhealthy and addictive behaviors.

Unfortunately, these behaviors to reduce stress actually increase it over the long term. That said, some entrepreneurs can perform successfully even if they do chain smoke, binge drink, eat unhealthily, or find other ways to medicate themselves, but they still cannot perform to their fullest potential or without a cost over time.

Now is the time for change, specifically healthy changes in our lives, companies, and communities. This change is imperative due to rising costs of healthcare, the overwhelming obesity epidemic (nearly 75% of American men and 60% of women are obese or overweight) and the stressors of our society leading to short lives. For instance, the US life expectancy dropped for the third year in a row, reflecting rising drug overdoses, suicides, and other deaths of despair.

Just ask Elon Musk. He's been known to log 80-, 100-, even 120-hour work weeks, and what did he have to say about it?

"It's not been great, actually," in typical Musk fashion.[26] His grueling schedule and lack of sleep has taken a toll on his well-being. But in our society, we look up to people like Musk—people who build empires, work on multiple projects, and never seem to stop.

For most of us, this standard for success seems impossible to keep up with. The message we often receive is to work until we drop, but this isn't sustainable for the long-term—nor should it be. If you have a strong handle on your Purpose Pillars, then you quickly realize that *being successful isn't all about work*. Wellness should—and can—be integrated into your purposeful journey. Wellness not only relieves stress, it brings us back to a sense of awareness in our minds and bodies and allows us to grow in new ways and make smarter choices.

According to Rashel Goldman, a Manhattan psychologist who specializes in stress reduction and weight management, "Health behaviors are the first thing to go when we are under stress."[27] We skip the gym, eat junk food, and fuel a downward spiral that drives unhealthy behavior up and performance down.

When stress is sky-high—like when dealing with messy office drama, missing a big product launch, or failing to raise money—we may just want to escape the pressure, leading us to indulge in bad habits.

We think these things make us feel better because they are immediate and they give us an instant hit of dopamine, but in reality, they are just exacerbating the problem and moving us further away from what we really need: to live through the discomfort of our emotions until we figure out what it is we really think and feel. When we allow ourselves to sit with our emotions (remember those?), we realize that the only reason we binge drink or eat too much or engage in unhealthy behaviors is to escape.

But when we allow ourselves to really tap into what we are feeling, we realize the worst thing that can happen is that we experience an emotion. That's it. It's not our actual shitty day that we're trying to escape—it's our *thoughts* about the shitty day that make us feel so out of control. When we pause in those situations, we can gain a sense of comfort and an element of control by letting those overwhelming destructive thoughts fade away and our purpose come back into focus, slowly helping us get back on our feet and take one step forward after another in a healthy way.

## TRAIN LIKE AN ATHLETE

While entrepreneurs don't train like elite athletes, your ability to perform is driven by the same factors that impact athletic performance. But unlike athletes, who typically compete in cycles and have off-seasons, entrepreneurs need to be game-ready *every day*. By using data to analyze stress levels, evaluate performance, and initiate recovery, entrepreneurs can ensure top performance on a daily basis.

To provide some personal evidence (other than throwing out my back), I took a look at the strain on my body from a hiking trip where I climbed four mountain passes carrying a 50-pound backpack. Then I compared that data to my work week prior to the trip. Although the total strain on my body from hiking trip was greater than during my work week, the strain from a high-stress workday that included no physical activity was surprisingly comparable to climbing up, over, and down a single mountain.

The Friday before my hiking trip, I had a "high-stakes meeting" that demanded a ton of energy and generated a lot of stress. As a result, my WHOOP daily strain score, which measures strain based on a variety of biometric data, was really high—it was equal to the last day of my hiking trip when I pounded out nine hours on the trial including summitting Buckskin Mountain (13,872'). Insane!

It's a small sample, but it does provide reasoning to reinforce the importance of recovery after a stressful work week. While I don't believe in the need to achieve a perfect balance, I do believe recovery is necessary to ensure top performance. I could show you hundreds of publications that support this thesis, ranging from studies of business executives to first responders to professional athletes.

We all have the same 24 hours in a day, from the most successful billionaires to the beach bums in Costa Rica. The way you spend your time is your decision (even when you don't feel like the choice is yours). Therefore, decide it is your priority. Make sure you are developing a routine for wellness—not an exception, not a distracted jaunt to the gym, but time for you every single day where you can unplug, process, move your body, meditate, or even just go for a walk with your partner. In doing so, you will reduce stress and also do something positive for mind, body, heart, and soul in the process.

If it helps, just think of your personal wellness as a critical part of your job, like an athlete. Treat it like a nonnegotiable (because that's what it is). Pay attention to daily habits, establish new healthy routines for yourself, and apply principles from your previous success to your own health to help you live at your best.

# ATTRACT GREAT FANS

In addition to being mental and physically well, start-up athletes need emotional support too, which aligns with the Love Purpose Pillar.

Keep in mind, the feedback of people close to us is important to be aware of, but it shouldn't sway us. Everyone has an opinion. It doesn't matter if no one understands your purpose or how you intend to use it. You don't need *permission* from anyone to do your thing.

Case in point: I asked my son (I won't reveal which one so as not to incriminate him) if he'd like to read my book when I finished, because I thought it would interest him.

*Him: I may skim it.*

*Me, incredulous: You wouldn't read it?*

*Him: I don't read a lot of books.*

*Me, mentally kicking myself for not making him read more books: Well, what if someone asked you if you've read my book? What would you say?*

*Him: I would tell them that I loved it and everyone should read it.*

*Me, to myself: Great, I've raised a liar. A supportive liar, but a liar nonetheless.*

The bottom line is this: it doesn't matter what others think about you living your version of a purposeful life. If they support it. If they don't support it. If they *pretend* to support it. *Just do it anyway.* You will never regret spending time customizing your life to your purpose. That said, create a team to help you be successful.

Surround yourself with people who really support you and aren't emotionally toxic or energetically draining. You want to align yourself with people who have the same values and believe in you and your goals. It's critical to your success. They will be there to support you when you fall, to help and encourage you to keep fighting. They will celebrate with you when you win, knowing the blood, sweat, and tears you put in.

Your fans may include your family, friends, or work colleagues, but be sure to terminate or distance yourself from people who are toxic to you or tell you what you can't, won't, or shouldn't do. You need to surround yourself with people who share your vision of success. They will help you, and you will help them to succeed and live at their best.

# BUILD A WINNING CULTURE

Furthermore, join teams, organizations, and companies that align with your Purpose Vision and Purpose Pillars. This allows you to be in an environment that will help you flourish. It will energize you, versus burning you out. In return, you will be performing at your best within your organization, ultimately delivering your best results, which improves the performance of the organization.

This is taking a Purpose First approach.

A Purpose First approach creates an environment for people to operate as their best selves. They are empowered to perform and live well. They provide the foundation to allow people to make choices to ensure they are mentally, physically, and emotionally healthy. The organization makes it part of the culture, but each individual has their own "it."

Keep in mind, a culture like this is not at odds with organization performance. Individuals are still accountable for their performance within an organization. They are still responsible for ensuring the organization hits its goals. However, they are in a better position to perform at their best and help their organization succeed because the organization is putting its people in the best position to be successful.

See, the paradigm has shifted. It's like an elite sports team. As a Purpose First Entrepreneur, you need to invest in your team of employees. Train them, energize them, and allow them to recover so they can produce sustainable results. Long gone are the days where managers grind people down and spit them out. Invest in them to get better results.

This doesn't mean there won't be long days or long weeks. There will be times when you have to dig in, get it done, and produce outstanding results. However, tireless work and relentless pressure just can't be the norm. Start-up athletes need to re-energize to work at their best over a sustainable period of time. Otherwise, they will be ground down and check out mentally or literally—they'll quit.

In his latest book, General Colin Powell explains that his vision of leadership rejects "busy bastards" who put in long hours at the office without realizing the impact they have on themselves and their staff. He explains that

> in every senior job I've had, I've tried to create an
> environment of professionalism and the very highest

standards. When it was necessary to get a job done, I expected my subordinates to work around the clock. When that was not necessary, I wanted them to work normal hours, go home at a decent time, play with the kids, enjoy family and friends, read a novel, clear their heads, daydream, and refresh themselves. I wanted them to have a life outside the office. I am paying them for the quality of their work, not for the hours they work. That kind of environment has always produced the best results for me.[28]

As General Powell illustrates, the organization's character is defined by the character of its leaders. The leaders are responsible for its culture. An organization's culture can be observed by how its people are or are not living its values.

The most sustainable teams and organizations have their own Purpose Vision and Purpose Pillars. At the heart of all it, the organization operates as one entity, putting the good of the group ahead of the individual. It is up to the individual to determine whether they can be their best self in serving the best of the organization. And it is up to the organization to determine whether it creates a platform that allows its people the ability to be their best.

Reshape your thinking. You are an elite start-up athlete. Train to perform like one. Your physical, mental, and emotional wellness has a direct impact on your performance, success, and happiness in every area of your life.

# CHAPTER 11

# PUTTING YOUR PURPOSE TO WORK

Congratulations. You created your Purpose Vision, established your Purpose Pillars, and started your Purpose First Business. You also learned how to harness your purpose to perform at an elite level as a start-up athlete. So, like any true champion, you must put in the daily work because that is where performance is perfected!

## ESTABLISH PURPOSEFUL ROUTINES

First, look inward and *connect with your purpose* each day. You know, the power that motivates you. Spend a few minutes mentally and emotionally tuning into your Purpose Vision and Purpose Pillars. You can meditate, recite your personal honor code, or journal about the impact of your Purpose Pillars. You can decide how to do it, whatever you feel is right for you that day, but be sure you connect with purpose on a *routine* basis.

Next, *schedule your priority Purpose Pillar* actions (e.g., *Wellness*: 10-minute morning meditation; *Wellness*: work out on Mon, Wed,

Thu, Sat, and Sun; *Love*: date night with wife on Fri). Don't feel you have to have every Pillar scheduled every week. But make sure you have at least one monthly action per Pillar. Schedule them on your calendar. Treat them like the most important meeting you will have that day. This *routine* locks the time down, significantly increases the probability of completion, and automates many recurring decisions. By blocking the time in advance, you move the decision process into the background, allowing you to focus your attention on other important matters.

Finally, create a system to divide big goals into manageable steps—*establish micro-goals*—this allows you to experience some success on a regular basis, which helps build momentum to reach the bigger goals.

Unfortunately for the majority of us, our goals often go unfulfilled because they're never broken down into easily digestible pieces.

Prioritize what three things you need to do that day to advance toward one or more of your top goals.

So?

Break.

Them.

Down.

The best part? Doing this only takes about five to ten minutes each day. That's less time than you spend waiting for your java at the local coffee joint.

I know it's not rocket science. But it does require personal accountability and willingness to create a *routine*. Liken it to brushing your teeth. When you miss a few days, your teeth are not going to fall out, but if you never brush them, they'll decay, yellow, and require more dental work than a 1960s hockey player's. Same with routines—miss a few days and the repercussions are hardly

> **❶ ATTENTION, PLEASE:** If you haven't done so already, go to PurposeFirstEntrepreneur.com/workbook to get the companion workbook. It is a great resource to help put your purpose to work.

noticeable. Over time, though, your goals will begin to rot because of lack of routine attention.

As the day or week winds down, take a moment to reflect on improving your performance. Did you achieve your goal(s)? Make a note: why or why not? Evaluate how you performed (ideally each day) against your micro-goal. This will allow you to track your performance and develop a Purposeful Improvement Loop (see Chapter 7) to reinforce the behavior you want.

Over time, you will be able to see how your progress toward long-term goals happens in daily increments. You get further insights if you add quick notes on your state of mind or what's impacting your performance, which may be positively or negatively impacting your progress. This allows for necessary insight to adjust your performance.

For those who are self-quantification enthusiasts like me, you can even turn this information into a helpful dashboard. Use an app (there are a lot out there) or create a simple, no-frills system to rate your daily performance using a spreadsheet. For example, +3 for excellent, +2 for good, +1 for okay, 0 for neutral, −1 for subpar, −2 for poor, −3 for very poor. Track your scores and look for patterns. Identifying patterns or trends of behavior over time will allow you to better hone your ability to improve. It's not meant to measure your worth, more to serve as a compass, guiding you on the path to becoming your best self.

You may even want to use your own types of personal rewards when you hit micro-goals, such as treating yourself to your favorite coffee. This allows for necessary insight and incentives to adjust your performance and be aligned with living and leading more purposefully.

# RETHINK WORK-LIFE BALANCE

Now you have a framework for building routines that help you tune into your purpose, elevate your performance, and reach your goals.

What about work-life balance?

I recommend rethinking the concept of "work-life balance." It is a standard that people can't live up to. After struggling with the pressure of trying to achieve it for years, I decided it focuses on the wrong outcome. I now take a personalized approach that's tied to my Purpose Pillars and is ultimately designed to help me be my best.

For me, there really is no such thing as a "typical day." The only thing that's typical is that days are usually full of purposeful activity. Since my days can get full quickly, I am diligent about planning my week to ensure that I can prioritize what is important to me and delegate or delete what is not.

I've found a lot of success in keeping my weeks fluid—there's no real beginning or end. I don't differentiate a Tuesday from a Saturday, for instance, just like I don't differentiate my career from my life. While this might mean I am "working" in some regard every day, that flexes up and down. As long as I do what's important to me to realize my Purpose Vision and live according to my Purpose Pillars—Honor, Love, Wellness, and Goodness—I feel comfortable with a seven-day "workweek." If you want clear demarcations of when you're working and when you're not, take the weekend off. Or work four days a week. You should do what is best for you. However, my work gives me energy because there is purpose in it.

Work, then, is definitely not separate from my life—it *is* my life (or at least a major component of it)—and my ability to balance my workload, day in and day out, is directly related to what I do to stay well and live well.

I like to begin each day with meditation, especially when I am really busy. I get it whenever and wherever I can. Sometimes this means meditating for a few minutes before a meeting or in my car in the parking lot. Just 10 minutes of mindful silence helps me to recalibrate and quiet any noises or distractions in my mind. I use a five-count technique that breathwork and sports-performance expert Matt Wilkins teaches his NFL, NBA, and PGA clients to improve their performance on the field. This routine helps get me into my Purpose First Mindset Zone, where my focus, awareness, and mindset are optimal. I don't always stay there, but when I'm not and need to be there, I go back to five-count breathing to get me back in the zone.

I also make a practice of regulating my sleep in three-day increments. Ideally, I would get at least seven hours of sleep a night, but this is not always doable. When sleep is cut short a couple of days in a row, I make sure to get seven-plus hours on the third day. I know that if I extend past that point, it will start to have an impact on me physically and mentally. Sleep is personal, so you have to find your optimal cycles. If you don't, there is no way you can perform at your best. Imagine if you were running a Spartan Ultra Race with nine hours sleep over the past three days—you would suck. Your performance would be a fraction of what it would be if you were well rested.

Other steps I take to prioritize my wellness include eating well, reducing alcohol consumption, and getting to the gym. During very busy times, I might reduce my time in the gym or just do bodyweight exercises, but I will rarely eliminate it altogether. If I do, my stress skyrockets and dramatically decreases my ability to focus on what's important. Bottom line—high stress impacts my ability to make good decisions. This can be a downward cycle: stress plus a series of bad decisions equals a lot more stress. If I don't infuse some rest, exercise, and interpersonal connections, it just keeps on repeating itself. I've learned this over time, so I commit to doing a little something, no matter how busy I am, to ensure I am doing the things that allow me to perform.

If I don't, stress seeps in and starts to corrode my relationships with people. I end up communicating poorly, being quick to criticize, or being very wrong when I think I'm very right. All of these stress-induced bad behaviors ultimately create bigger problems with my friends, family, and colleagues, which creates more stress that consumes even more of my time than if I'd simply taken some time for myself to reduce my stress level.

And when things are stressful to the point of mental and physical fatigue? I know it's time to take a break. And I quickly do. You would stop if you broke your arm, because if you didn't, the damage would get worse and eventually become irreparable. This can happen at work or in life if you don't take a break when you're overwhelmed with stress. Take a nap, call a good friend, or go on vacation. (You get the idea.) I often take a hot whirlpool with Epsom salt. This allows me to soothe tense muscles (from the stress) and clear my mind from the hurricane of noise (e.g., what someone did, the deal that fell apart, etc.) and refocus on what matters (my Purpose Vision and Purpose Pillars). It also helps me to sleep better, which is the best remedy for just about anything.

Everyone has their own way of going about their work and balancing priorities. What works for me, as I've shared, may not work for everyone, and I get that. But I also believe there are broader concepts that can be applied universally and may help to lessen the toll of stress during busy times.

So, enough already—today is the first day of the rest of your life! Don't fret about yesterday or worry about tomorrow. Wherever you are, whatever time of day it is, make it happen! Focus on being your best today. Put your purpose to work!

# CHAPTER 12

# NOW IS THE TIME!

Is now the time to become a Purpose First Entrepreneur? Maybe someone in your family or one of your friends is telling you how risky it is. Or just you're too afraid to move forward with your dream of starting a new business.

These are certainly uncertain times. Many of us assume we should wait until things are more certain before we make an entrepreneurial move, right?

Well, if you'd asked a wide selection of my friends and colleagues on New Year's Day in 2020 how the year was going to turn out, they were *100%* certain that 2020 was going to be the best year ever. They would talk about their jobs, businesses, health, and tell you that life was literally firing on all cylinders. Most expected 2020 to be a banner year.

Fast-forward just a few months, and their lives were turned upside down. As a matter of fact, a lot of my friends and colleagues saw their businesses shuttered. The pandemic left a wake of economic fallout that we are still recovering from. In addition, many of these same people are faced with the health-related impact of COVID-19—either being sick themselves or supporting family and friends who have to deal with loved ones passing away or being intubated, then facing a long road to recovery.

What happened in 2020 is exactly why I wrote this book. Life is often uncontrollable. However, we do control what is important to us *if* we pay attention to what truly matters on a regular basis. Our Purpose Pillars give us the foundation to navigate good times (to enjoy them more) and lousy times (to give us the strength to get up, dust ourselves off, and start fighting again). Being aligned with your Purpose Vision makes sure every moment is meaningful from a business perspective but, more importantly, from a life perspective.

There is no 100% certain path. So given that, why not take a risk? As we've quite literally seen, no one is guaranteed tomorrow, and we certainly don't want to regret not trying. Bet on yourself. Do the work to mitigate the risks. And align your life with your values and start a business that gets you out of bed early, ready to kick ass and own your life with the decisions you make.

It really does work out. And that takes some getting used to. Because so many of us are taught not to expect it, but we all deserve to enjoy the fruits of our labor. As things start rolling, you may hit a bump or two (or maybe three). But any great success takes time. You eventually get some momentum. The Purpose First Performance Equation will help you continuously improve and help you reach your goals. Your Purpose Pillars will provide the foundation and, if properly maintained, allow you to enjoy the journey along the way.

If I had to pick one thing in life that I would want everyone to have, I would give them a big infusion of resilience and a huge dose of persistence. These will not guarantee success in business, but they will guarantee success in life. The methodologies, equations, and practices covered in this book will help you use those traits to live your best life.

Your soul is filled with a never-ending supply of purpose. The purpose is to live your best life and make a huge difference in the world, in your own special way. However, the flame that keeps purpose burning in your soul can go out. And it takes a lot of personal fortitude to restart it after you get knocked down. We will all get knocked down. Hell, I may be the king of getting knocked down, but I always get up. And so should you, because failure is necessary to live our best lives.

Ironically, when I meet people for the first time in business settings, they compliment me on my success. They have likely read my LinkedIn profile or glanced at my bio at the back of the book or heard me present at a start-up conference and made some assumptions about me. They ask, "How did you do it?" They think that I skillfully navigated the entrepreneurial landscape without hitting any landmines and that I have all the answers.

Even though I have experienced some incredible successes, I've also experienced some really painful failures and setbacks, both personally and professionally. Those feelings—you know the ones that can gnaw at your gut and make you feel like you might barf or that bring tears to your eye—can be debilitating and may alter your life forever. But don't let them. Get up. Brush yourself off. And try again.

Resilience matters. Overcoming failure matters. Trying matters. Action is exactly what puts you on the path to success. Be empowered. Don't let setbacks take you out. Learn what's important to you and why. Know what energizes and who energizes you. Knowing this will power you as a Purpose First Entrepreneur to build a business and life that matters.

As a Purpose First Entrepreneur, it's your job to see opportunities. Big ones. The world is changing. Capture your opportunity. Launch your Purpose First Business. Make it happen. Like I often say, I would much rather fail than fail to try. More importantly, you will never be successful at building a Purpose First Business if you don't try.

You have a real opportunity to create a legacy that matters. One that will be defined by you. Your Purpose. Your Purpose Pillars. Your Purpose First Mindset. You will put a stamp on the world that says, *I made a difference*!

Go live a Purpose First life. Demonstrate it in the way you live, feel, act, run your business, and nourish relationships with others. Although you won't be perfect, and you'll have your fair share of setbacks, you will one day look back on your life fondly. You'll be satisfied. You'll know that you took control of the things that mattered to you and let go of the things you couldn't control.

Wherever you are in the process, understand that these tools are always available to you. All you have to do is tap in, make the decision, and lead with purpose.

You've got this.

# PROOF IT WORKS

## PUTTING IT TO THE TEST

Establishing a Purpose First Mindset infuses the power of purpose into what we do. It allows us to achieve unbelievable success and to overcome seemingly insurmountable obstacles.

Just a few months before this book went to print, the universe decided to slap me upside my head (figuratively and literally). She said, *Hellooo*! We are going to test you and your *Purpose First Entrepreneur* principles, methodologies, and guidance. We are going to test you big time, and from different angles than when you were younger. Like checking to see whether a well-seasoned pier can withstand the brutal forces of a hurricane. Will you still be standing after the storm is gone? Will *Purpose First Entrepreneur* really deliver?

Well … The test started off smoothly at first. As a matter of fact, 2021 started off very well. I felt there was a certain synchronicity with the universe. The wind was at my back and successes kept rolling in. Entrepreneurs that I knew well, who embraced the Purpose First Mindset and infused it into their companies and lives, were achieving unprecedented business successes.[29] They were joining the super-exclusive Unicorn Club.[30]

These Purpose First Entrepreneurs' successes helped validate the model. However, some big personal challenges, which were totally out of my control and came seemingly out of nowhere, would challenge me to my very core. These life-changing successes and life-threatening challenges that were happening simultaneously gave me a clear idea of the test I was taking. Would I pass?

Whether I was ready or not, I was about to find out.

## HOW A GOOD DAY TURNED REALLY BAD

In late April, I got up, ready to enjoy the weekend. I completed my morning routine. All was good. My health was never better. Things in my life were operating all on cylinders.

Life was good.

Suddenly, everything changed. I was having trouble talking and moving normally. It seemed, in a matter of hours, my body simply stopped working right. I didn't know what was going on, but I needed to get to the emergency room.

My son helped my wife get me into the car. We assumed it would be a rather "routine ER visit" (meaning in and out without any big issues). Given our family dynamic, there were even a few jokes about me having trouble walking and talking—obviously I was over the hill or maybe I shouldn't have had that third martini with breakfast.

By Sunday evening, I was intubated, sedated, and fighting for my life. There was swelling in my brain, which was shutting down my capacity for my body to properly function. It wasn't a stroke. It wasn't meningitis. It wasn't COVID-19. The doctors truly didn't know *what* it was, but they knew there was a life-threatening emergency. They needed to decrease the swelling in my brain, pronto. The next 48 hours would be critical.

My wife left the hospital at 3:00 a.m. thinking I might not make it. Emotionally drained, physically exhausted, and unclear about the future, she broke down and cried as she sat in our car in the parking lot. The next day, she told my teenage sons about what was going on and the critical nature of my condition. She knew that she had to prepare them for the worst, given the current circumstances.

Throughout the first few days, my wife started to reach out to family and friends to let them know and create a network of support for us. She also alerted my work colleagues, so they were aware personally to be supportive but would also make sure no balls were dropped in my absence. It catalyzed the emotional support of loving relationships that I would need to get through this, which clearly ties to the importance of the Purpose Pillar of Love.

As time went by, my condition stabilized. I was off the ventilator and no longer sedated. Everyone's stress levels dropped a notch. However, the doctors were still unclear what was causing my brain inflammation. I was going through a battery of blood tests, lumbar punctures, MRIs ... Basically you name it, it was being tested to try to determine the cause of my condition.

The preliminary tests ruled out all of the typical causes. I was in good shape cognitively. However, my motor skills weren't, especially my lower body.

In other words, I could no longer walk.

Just a few weeks earlier, I was killing my workouts and planning for my annual mountain hiking trip. Now I couldn't even stand on my own, let alone on top of a mountain. While I was shocked and devastated, I finally tapped into my Purpose First Mindset.

This was the ultimate test. Did I believe in what I was teaching others? Could I apply it to any situation, especially my own?

Yes, I could. So I did.

I told myself: *Here is where you are. Where do you want to go?* I decided to develop a plan to get there. I cleared my mind of the past. I didn't focus on *why* this happened to me. It didn't matter. I knew I could only control what I was going to do next.

And that next critical step was to get my legs working.

It was time to get me out of the medical hospital and get to a hospital that could focus on getting me walking again. I was transported to an inpatient rehabilitation hospital, which is a hospital devoted to the rehabilitation of patients after their acute medical issues have stabilized. Five hours later, I was in an ambulance back to the medical hospital. Six hours later, I was back in the emergency room. Ten hours later, I was back in the ICU. The doctors had detected a flare-up of the brain inflammation and determined my body was the cause. My body was actually attacking itself, which is an autoimmune-related condition. They still didn't know the exact cause, but they knew the broader category, which helped target the medical treatment options, which they started immediately. Fast-forward about a week, and the medical treatment started to make a difference, and off I went back to the rehabilitation hospital.

At the rehabilitation hospital, the progress was slow. My walking, balance, and strength improved a little each day, but I became more and more fatigued. There was pressure building in my head from the back of my skull to behind my eyes. It was causing severe headaches and impacting my vision. By the tenth day at the rehabilitation hospital, I hit a wall that literally stopped me in my tracks.

I pushed myself up and out of my wheelchair anyway. I gained my balance. I told my physical therapist that I was really, really fatigued but I would try my best in our session. I was determined to make some progress. A little would be OK. A little progress was better than no progress. I took one small step, the second, and barely a third. Boom! I start to fold like a wet noodle. I was collapsing to the floor, but on the way down, I grabbed my physical therapist to slow my fall. Luckily, she was prepared. She had me draped over her left shoulder and gently guided me back into my wheelchair.

As my therapist sat me in my wheelchair, I was crushed. I was exhausted, defeated, and felt like shit. She wheeled me back to my room. My younger son was in my room (keep in mind due to COVID-19 protocol, he rarely got to see me. And most times, I made sure I was in good spirits. This time, not so much). He was alarmed by my state as things once again seemed to be turning toward the worst-case scenario.

This downturn was tough on me. However, I wasn't giving up. I was battling, doing my best, regardless of the situation. This lesson, this experience, was directly tied to my purpose and my Purpose Pillars. As a dad, this was really important to me, regardless of my health circumstances. I was showing leadership to my sons, not only in good times, but also in the hardest times. I had developed some "muscle memory" from the past in overcoming previous challenging situations, which helped me a lot.

The uncertainty of our circumstances and its impact on our ability to perform, ultimately affecting our ability to reach our goals, is something entrepreneurs deal with all the time. The more aware of your circumstances, the more likely you are to decide to adjust your performance to reach your goals. In my case, I knew patience and persistence were critical to allow the medical treatment to work and put me in a position to go all out in rehab to get better.

I kept reminding myself to do my best with what I had right then, and that I would eventually be okay. When the doctor finally came into my hospital room, my physical therapist had already debriefed him. The doctor thoroughly evaluated me. Both my legs were shot, and my left foot wasn't moving at all. He told me and my son he was concerned there may be another flare-up. He was sending me back to the medical hospital immediately. So, back in the ambulance to the emergency room for even more CT scans, MRIs, lumbar punctures, lab tests, etc. Electrodes were attached to my chest, an IV jabbed in my arm. I felt like a pincushion. It was getting to be a new routine ... one that never led anywhere definitive.

They compared my new information with my previous information. They had a better sense of what they needed to treat. They also determined what was causing the pressure in my head, which was impacting my vision and creating piercing headaches. Now it was a matter of selecting a second treatment option that would work.

# RECLAIMING PURPOSE

That night, I reflected on my new daunting journey. It was like my entire life was being experienced at retro-hyperspace speed over the previous month or so. However, this new journey was still a *hard ass* test. Honestly, I wasn't sure I was going to pass. I think many entrepreneurs can relate as they face big obstacles in their journeys.

This wasn't the first time I'd faced a major life-threatening health situation. Nearly half my life ago, I faced a similar battle to stay alive and ultimately find my purpose.

> *When I was in college, I was violently attacked. I bore the force of a baseball player swinging a bat at a 100-mph fastball. The blow shattered my skull and punctured an artery in my brain. Blood gushed from the open wound as I fell to the floor. I was rushed to the emergency room, and the doctors told my friends and family to hope for a miracle. After two brain surgeries—one that required a plate in my skull—I had an arduous recovery. I had to learn how to walk, talk, and cognitively function again. It was a miracle I even survived, but I did!*

Now, nearly thirty years later, I was facing another arduous recovery. My experience in life and as an entrepreneur taught me a lot about overcoming life's biggest challenges. When you are faced with seemingly insurmountable odds, reclaiming your purpose pushes you to survive.

However, my Purpose First Mindset wasn't there that evening. Being in the hospital and still not truly knowing what was happening was the ultimate test in surrendering to what was and wasn't in my control. But I had been on a similar road before, and I fought back. *Came* back.

Now I just had to do it again.

We all experience challenges in life. We may want to give up.

We want to quit or stop trying. But in the end, we need a reason to survive. We need hope. We need a why. We need purpose. This makes us fight for what matters.

The back-and-forth between giving up and getting up battled in my head as the night went on. So I calibrated my Purpose First Mindset. I got focused on what mattered. I was aware of the current situation. And I finally got my mind right.

I reclaimed my purpose. It was anchored in improving my health. Although, it was more than just health; it was centered on what I was living for. It was much greater than me. It was for my family: my wife and my sons. Peeling it back further, the motivation really stemmed from my Purpose Pillars, specifically being driven by the Purpose Pillar of Honor. My personal code of honor: "*I am committed to leading my life with Honor by treating others and myself with Respect, acting with Integrity, and always Doing My Best.*"

When your circumstances are good, decisions are easier. However, I try to teach my sons that there are important decisions that will need to be made in unfavorable circumstances, which will have a big impact on your life. Many times the circumstances change and you have no control of them, so you're forced to the best with the options you have. This is true for everyone, especially entrepreneurs. As everyone knows, that sucks. It's unfair. Right?

Well, I am not sure who determines fair or not. But life isn't fair *or* unfair. It's life. And it's your decision regarding the path you choose to take moving forward. Furthermore, your success will have a lot to do with your mindset once you make it. Both are decisions you get to make.

In my current health condition, my goal is to set an enduring example of how to make the decisions for my two sons as they become adults. I aspire to help them establish Purpose Pillars that will be a foundation for their lives. This is especially motivating to me because my dad died when I was just about their age. He was my best friend and instilled many of my core values in me. Unfortunately, as I became an adult, a husband, and a father, he wasn't able to continue imparting his wisdom. Although he could not do that for me, I wanted to make sure I could do that for my sons.

I want to reinforce the importance of Purpose Pillars to *all* entrepreneurs. Regardless of your business priorities, you can't shortcut your Pillar development. You must follow your personal *honor* code, nurture *loving* relationships, commit to your *wellness*, and participate in the creation of *goodness* in the world. My Purpose Pillars have certainly helped me throughout my life to make it richer, but when I was lost during my worst times, they propped me up and kept me going.

The Purpose Pillar of Love and the importance of meaningful connection is paramount. I will tell you that my family, friends, colleagues, and other community relationships powered my recovery. They made me feel whole, even though I felt broken into emotional, mental, and physical pieces. For those entrepreneurs reading, take it from me, be absolutely sure to dedicate time to nurture those relationships along your start-up journey. The true, authentic, loving relationships you have with people will make your business better and your life richer.

My Purpose Pillars provided me the foundation to reclaim my purpose. They helped me weather the storm and ultimately get back on track. Not where I thought was going to be in the past or where I wanted to be in the future. But here I am, in the moment, alive and equipped to be the best I can be.

## TESTED, PASSED, AND PROVEN!

Finally, the doctors were starting to figure out what was wrong with me: they believed it was *autoimmune encephalitis,* a collection of related conditions in my body's immune system that were attacking my brain. However, they still didn't know the direct cause. Once I had an understanding of the condition, at least, it was time to work my ass off to get better, one day at a time. This meant my goals had to change, and how I performed to achieve them needed to be modified; they needed to align with my new circumstances.

This is the same problem Purpose First Entrepreneurs face. Circumstances drastically change. Then you have to adjust your performance to reach your goals. This reinforces the Purpose First Performance Equation.

During my stay in the hospital, a lot was also going on at my firm that made me think of trials and tribulations we all face. I was thinking about the journey of Ed Bellis. We were one of the first investors in the company he co-founded. His journey wasn't bump free; however, he persevered and built it into an incredible business. In June 2021, Cisco officially announced the acquisition of his company, Kenna Security, which unified both companies' platforms to become the market leader in risk-based vulnerability cybersecurity management. It was an awesome outcome, which inspired me.

Ed's journey made me challenge myself. So did the experiences of so many other entrepreneurs I knew very well who'd reached "unicorn" status over the previous few months. They all embraced the Purpose First Entrepreneur approach. They demonstrated how purpose gives us the motivation, resilience, and power to fight for what matters to us to be our best.

Inspired and ready, I knew what needed to be done. Hell, I wrote a book on it! First, I established new goals and created new routines. I broke my goals down into manageable chunks. Although I would have setbacks, none caused me to want to give up, thanks to my Purpose First Mindset. As a result, I made progress. My ability to walk improved, and I was getting slightly better every day.

As my second medical treatment was starting to take effect, momentum was shifting. It was almost like someone just turned the light switch from off to on! My balance was improving, my energy levels were up, the fatigue was gone, my eyesight returned to normal, and I had no more headaches. The doctors were stoked. This treatment was working.

I had a new sense of confidence. The doctors thought it might take longer than I expected, and I was likely going to need some assistance walking, such as a wheelchair or walker. At this point, I didn't care what I needed, as long as I was getting better and finally getting home.

I was improving on all fronts. I could get myself ready for the day without help. (Meaning, I could balance myself to brush my teeth, shave, put my socks on one foot at a time, that kind of stuff.) Then, they checked specific body functions: Was I swallowing (previously, I was having food going down the wrong pipe, which is bad)? Then they wanted to make sure I was cognitively aware and operating on all cylinders. Check! Looking good. Everything was a go!

My physical therapy was progressing. It went from my therapist supporting me to achieving a personal best for walking by myself. After I hit my PBR, my legs were shaking like a tall building during an earthquake, but I was full of confidence and hopeful about my future.

I was turning the corner. As a Purpose First Entrepreneur, you may experience a similar journey. Your start-up is going well. An unforeseen, uncontrollable event occurs, your business looks like it's going to crater, you lose, then reclaim, your purpose, pivot your business given the new circumstances, and your business resurrects itself based on your new plan, and becomes even better than before. You gain momentum and start seeing success become the norm.

That was me. And things started to rapidly progress. I went from just walking, to walking on the treadmill on an incline with ankle weights, to walking on an incline with ankle weights with a physical therapist pulling on a belt around my waist. Eventually, I was doing ladder drills that you see soccer or football players doing to improve their footwork. (I don't want to paint the wrong picture: I was still slow putting each foot down, and I needed a physical therapist to be near me, but I was doing it!)

It seemed like a quantum leap forward every day. My vision was good. My energy was good. My humor was back (well, if you thought I ever had it in the first place). It was awesome. The struggles I had been facing were fading, and the successes were building.

Fast-forward: I was finally released from the rehabilitation hospital three weeks earlier than expected. I went home. Family and friends celebrated. I had no restrictions on what I could do or not do. I was self-sufficient. I was walking on my own without a problem. No wheelchair or walker needed! Hurrah!

My neurologist—who specializes in autoimmune encephalitis—refined my diagnosis to ADEM (Acute Disseminated Encephalomyelitis)/AIDP (Inflammatory Demyelinating Polyradiculopathy, commonly known as Guillain-Barré Syndrome). Both are related conditions that can be caused by vaccines in a very rare number of people (think of the likelihood of a start-up becoming a "unicorn," and there you go).

As my doctor told me this news, it began to make sense. I'd received the Johnson & Johnson COVID-19 vaccine two weeks before my symptoms appeared, and early that week, before my doctor visit, J&J had reported that men matching my profile experienced similar symptoms.[31] She explained that we needed a little more data before she was 100% confident this was the cause, but she felt it likely was.

The good news is my neurologist believes it is a one-and-done episode, and it will not be a chronic condition. Although I am still participating in physical therapy and being monitored to ensure there are no flare-ups of my condition, I am progressing nicely and looking good on all fronts. Despite my negative reaction to the vaccine, I want to make it clear, I support getting vaccinated. My case is extremely rare, and the overall good of the vaccine for global health is enormous. The personal sacrifices that I had to make for the "better good" of society are directly aligned with my purpose and Purpose Pillars, so I know I am living my values regardless of what life gives me.

I am unsure what will unfold in the future for me, but I am confident the lessons *Purpose First Entrepreneur* set forth helped me navigate this traumatic experience to be my best self and manifest success in my life regardless of the circumstances. I am equally confident it will help you too!

If I've learned anything, it's this: having a Purpose First Mindset allows us to overcome the challenges we face along the journey. Stormy times are buffered by strong Purpose Pillars, which provide the resilience we need to get up, dust ourselves off, and fight another day.

I hope, wherever you are, whatever your challenge, you will join me—and always lead with purpose along the way.

## Thank you for reading my book.

If you found it helpful, I'd deeply appreciate it if you took a few minutes to **share *Purpose First Entrepreneur* with your friends on social media** or write a review on the site where you purchased your copy. Reviews from readers like you are critical and make a big difference, one post at a time.

# NOTES

1   Quoted in "Vestar Capital Partners to Make Minority Investment in Simple
    Mills," Vestar Capital Partners, published October 7, 2019, http://www.
    vestarcapital.com/vestar-capital-partners-to-make-minority-investment-in-
    simple-mills.

2   For more information about Future Founders, visit their website: https://www.
    futurefounders.com.

3   "Prediabetes—Your Chance to Prevent Type 2 Diabetes," Centers for Disease
    Control and Prevention, last updated June 11, 2020, https://www.cdc.gov/
    diabetes/basics/prediabetes.html; "Diabetes Statistics," Diabetes Research
    Institute, https://www.diabetesresearch.org/diabetes-statistics, accessed June 18,
    2021.

4   Tori Marsh, "Depression and Anxiety Prescriptions Are Climbing Nationwide,"
    *Good Rx*, published May 2, 2019, https://www.goodrx.com/blog/depression-and-
    anxiety-prescriptions-are-climbing-nationwide.

5   G2 is a technology marketplace that allows businesses to review products and
    services. You can find them at https://www.g2.com/.

6   "42 Worrying Workplace Stress Statistics," The American Institute of Stress,
    published September 25, 2019, https://www.stress.org/42-worrying-workplace-
    stress-statistics.

7   You can find great free resources for entrepreneurs at sites like https://www.
    entrepreneur.com, https://www.inc.com, https://review.firstround.com, https://
    a16z.com.

8   You can connect with 500 Start-ups at https://500.co, and YCombinator at
    https://www.ycombinator.com.

9   You can connect with Future Founders at https://www.futurefounders.com,
    TECHRISE at https://techrise.co, Yellow at https://www.yellowla.com, GET Cities
    at https://www.getcities.org, and Bunker Labs at https://bunkerlabs.org.

10  You can connect with American Inno at https://www.bizjournals.com/inno,
    Startup Grind at https://www.startupgrind.com/, and TechCrunch at https://
    techcrunch.com.

11  You can connect with the SBA at https://www.sba.gov/.

12  For information on the DOE's investment in vehicle technology, see Office of
    Energy Efficiency and Renewable Energy, "DOE Announces $60 Million to
    Accelerate Advanced Vehicle Technologies Research," published December
    10, 2020, https://www.energy.gov/eere/articles/doe-announces-60-million-
    accelerate-advanced-vehicle-technologies-research. You can get more

information about federal grants and search current grant opportunities at https://www.grants.gov/web/grants.

13 You can connect with P33 at https://p33chicago.com/, with Discovery Partner Institute at https://dpi.ui llinois.edu/, with Northwestern's The Garage at https:// thegarage.northwestern.edu, with the University of Chicago Polsky Center at https://polsky.uchicago.edu, with 1871 at https://1871.com, with Matter at https://matter.health, with Portal Innovations at https://www.portalinnovations. com, and with The Hatchery at https://thehatcherychicago.org.

14 You can connect with OurCrowd at https://www.ourcrowd.com, with AngelList at https://angel.co, and with Silicon Valley bank at https://www.svb.com.

15 You can find the Angel Capital Association member directory at https://www. angelcapitalassociation.org/directory.

16 You can find and connect with your NVCA regional group at https://nvca.org/ resources/regional-groups.

17 Paul Gompers et al., "How Venture Capitalists Make Decisions," *Harvard Business Review*, March–April 2021, https://hbr.org/2021/03/how-venture-capitalists-make-decisions.

18 *Department of Homeland Security* v. *Regents of Univ. of Cal.*, 591 U. S. (2020), https://www.supremecourt.gov/opinions/19pdf/18-587_5ifl.pdf.

19 Reproduced with permission from Garry Cooper, "Minority Business Enterprise (MBE) Certifications Needs a Simple Fix," *Forbes*, published June 9, 2020, https:// www.forbes.com/sites/forbesbusinesscouncil/2020/06/09/minority-business-enterprise-mbe-certification-needs-a-simple-fix/?sh=61cc5f05e0af.

20 *Bostock* v. *Clayton County*, 590 U. S. (2020), https://www.supremecourt.gov/ opinions/19pdf/17-1618_hfci.pdf.

21 As quoted in Richard Wolf, "Supreme Court Grants Federal Job Protections to Gay, Lesbian, Transgender Workers," *USA Today*, published June 15, 2020, https://www.usatoday.com/story/news/politics/2020/06/15/supreme-court-denies-job-protection-lgbt-workers/4456749002/.

22 Ariane de Vogue and Devan Cole, "Supreme Court Says Federal Law Protects LGBTQ Workers from Discrimination," CNN, published June 15, 2020, https:// www.cnn.com/2020/06/15/politics/supreme-court-lgbtq-employment-case/ index.html.

23 Alphonso David, Twitter post, June 15, 2020, 9:27 a.m., https://twitter.com/ AlphonsoDavid/status/1272536304681717762.

24 Dan Mager, "Mindfulness and Emotional Intelligence," Psychology Today, published March 22, 2019, https://www.psychologytoday.com/us/blog/some-assembly-required/201903/mindfulness-and-emotional-intelligence.

25 Bojana Galic, "126 Running Statistics You Need to Know," Livestrong, published

February 18, 2021, https://www.livestrong.com/article/13730338-running-statistics.

26 As quoted in David Gelles et al., "Elon Musk Details 'Excruciating' Personal Toll of Tesla Turmoil," *The New York Times*, published August 16, 2018, https://www.nytimes.com/2018/08/16/business/elon-musk-interview-tesla.html.

27 Quoted in Kate Rope, "How Stress Makes Us Gain," in "The Science of Weight Loss," special issue, *Time* (January 2019).

28 Colin Powell with Tony Kotlz, *It Worked for Me: In Life and Leadership* (New York: HarperCollins, 2012), 40. I first encountered this passage and Powell's phrase "busy bastards" in Sheryl Sandberg's *Lean In: Women, Work, and the Will to Lead* (New York: Knopf Doubleday Publishing Group, 2013).

29 That list includes Godard Abel, Co-founder & CEO, G2; Kristi Ross, Co-CEO & President, tastytrade; Jason VandeBoom, Founder & CEO, ActiveCampaign; and Divey Gulati and Dhruv Saxena, Co-Founders, ShipBob.

30 To become a "unicorn," a start-up needs to reach a valuation of $1 billion or more.

31 Cases of the Guillain-Barré Syndrome have been seen in some people who got the J&J COVID-19 vaccine. Health authorities have found about 100 reports of the disorder among the 12.8 million people in the US who have taken the shot, according to the Centers for Disease Control and Prevention. Most of the reports, the agency added, came two weeks after vaccination among men 50 years and older. The warning label says that most cases appeared within 42 days of vaccination. Guillain-Barré is a rare side effect of some other vaccines and occurs very rarely in the general population. See Jenny Strasburg and Parmy Olson, "J&J, AstraZeneca Explore Covid-19 Vaccine Modification in Response to Rare Blood Clots," *The Wall Street Journal,* July 13, 2021, https://www.wsj.com/articles/j-j-astrazeneca-explore-covid-19-vaccine-modification-in-response-to-rare-blood-clots-11626173015?mod=article_inline; Janssen Therapeutics, "Fact Sheet for Recipients and Caregivers: Emergency Use Authorization (EUA) of the Janssen COVID-19 Vaccine to Prevent Coronavirus Disease 2019 (COVID-19) in Individuals 18 Years of Age and Older," updated as of July 8, 2021, https://www.fda.gov/media/146305/download; Felicia Schwartz, "Guillain-Barré Syndrome and the J&J Vaccine: What to Know and What Are the Risks," *The Wall Street Journal,* July 13, 2021, https://www.wsj.com/articles/guillain-barre-syndrome-j-j-vaccine-11626190624.

# ABOUT THE AUTHOR

There is no doubt Pete Wilkins knows what it means to have purpose. During the pandemic, Pete's body shut down; he was intubated, sedated, and forced to fight for his life. He won that battle.

But it was his war to stay alive as a teenager that first taught him the power of purpose. When he was 10 years old, Pete's mother died of cancer. A few years later, his father had a heart attack on the day of his high school homecoming and died 18 months later from a stroke. Less than a year after his father's death, Pete was brutally attacked. He was clubbed in the head so violently, the right side of his skull was completely shattered. He nearly died before he even reached the hospital (let alone his twentieth birthday). As a result, Pete was frequently forced to contemplate the purpose of life. He became a fighter. His purpose was not only to survive, but to *thrive*, which has guided the trajectory of his life.

He learned to grow his entrepreneurial spirit and dedicate his life to the pursuit of his own purpose.

Before he was 30, Pete was a critical part of two technology start-ups that sold and IPO-ed for more than $2.8 billion. He later went on to lead the turnaround of a medical education company from record losses to record profits, which he followed by starting a double-bottom-line company focused on college attainment for Latino families. Not every step was successful, but they were all purposeful.

Today, Pete leads HPA—one of the most successful early-stage venture investor groups in the country. He and his firm have partnered with hundreds of founders to help turn their dreams into reality, helping them scale their businesses from start-ups into industry leaders, many of which have gone on to join the exclusive "Unicorn Club." As a venture investor, board member, and advisor to many entrepreneurs, Pete has created billions of dollars of economic value, but more importantly, he has helped countless founders manifest their purposes into thriving businesses that are improving the world.

In the spirit of giving back, Pete shares his perspective and insights about investing in companies and people as a contributor for *Forbes* and Thrive Global. He is also passionate about building his local community and is actively engaged in leadership roles in multiple Chicago entrepreneurial, civic, and nonprofit organizations. In recognition of his contributions, Pete has been named one of the Top 100 Chicago Innovators by *The Chicago Tribune* and 50 on Fire by *ChicagoInno*. He's the winner of Illinois Technology Association's CityLIGHTS Industry Champion Award and the Chicago Innovation Award.

Pete holds a degree in business from Indiana University and graduated from the University of Chicago Booth Executive Institute. He resides in Chicago with his family.

# PURPOSE FIRST ENTREPRENEUR

Want to put everything you learned into practice and keep on learning? Go to **PurposeFirstEntrepreneur.com/workbook.**

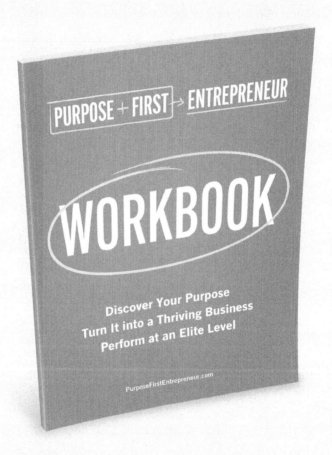

## Workbook for Purpose First Entrepreneur

**Download the companion workbook.** It is a great resource to help you organize your thoughts, translate them into actions, and turn those actions into a thriving business and life.

Made in the USA
Middletown, DE
28 October 2021